Keys to Solution in
BRIEF THERAPY

Keys to Solution in BRIEF THERAPY

Steve de Shazer
Director
Brief Family Therapy Center/
Wisconsin Institute on Family Studies
Milwaukee, Wisconsin

W·W·NORTON & COMPANY
New York   *London*

Published simultaneously in Canada by Penguin Books Canada Ltd,
2801 John Street, Markham, Ontario L3R 1B4.

Printed in the United States of America.

Library of Congress Cataloging in Publication Data

De Shazer, Steve.
 Keys to solution in brief therapy.

 Bibliography: p.
 Includes index.
 1. Psychotherapy, Brief. I. Title.
RC480.55.D4 1985   616.89'14   84-22781

ISBN 0-393-70004-6

W. W. Norton & Company, Inc., 500 Fifth Avenue, New York, NY 10110

W. W. Norton & Company Ltd., 37 Great Russell Street, London WC1B 3NU

8 9 0

FOREWORD

John H. Weakland

This book by Steve de Shazer is worth reading – as well as being easier to read than some of his prior writing – and I would like to use this foreword to say why I think so.

I will pitch this explanation mainly at a rather broad and general level, for two reasons. Despite constant pleas from puzzled or harried practitioners wanting specific solutions to specific problems, I believe that significant advances in practice depend primarily on developments in general views about problems and their resolution. And despite de Shazer's numerous and useful specific illustrative case vignettes, to me the essence of his book lies in its general views and propositions.

In reading this book, I found it contained a striking combination of points, old and new, with which I could readily agree from my own work, and important others where I disagreed or at least had initial reservations. On further thought, I see this apparent difficulty or contradiction as potentially highly positive, especially if it is considered in the framework of "poly-ocular viewing" which de Shazer (following Bateson) himself advocates. That is, if two related but different views of a given matter exist (whether the particular situation involves two team members observing a case, two approaches to problem resolution, or indeed, and most basic to our whole field, two family members describing a problem differently), this offers a possibility for the emergence of a "bonus." That is, essentially, a higher-level and integrative view can result, if one can avoid the trap of "Which is the *right* view?" Thus, I see de Shazer as offering us, not – God forbid! – final answers, but further help in escaping from the limitations of "knowing what ain't so" and defending our partial truths with

v

the same sort of desperate insistence that we see our patients display for *theirs*.

More specifically, he offers, among other things, an expansion of our horizons by an emphasis on solutions as a counterweight to previous emphasis on the origins or the nature of problems, an expansion of one's vision of "cooperation" in therapy as contrasted to "resistance," including ideas about how to work with those vague clients who are otherwise the bane of strategic therapists, and some seminal thoughts on "formula" interventions. These last, together with the recent work of Mara Selvini-Palazzoli, may well mark an important new step. Now that we have broken down older, unuseful general categories of diagnosis and therapy by examining the specifics of problems and treatment using an interactional view, it may be time to begin generalizing again, more usefully.

In short, for those who are not too obsessed with demanding specific and immediate answers, and can accept that it is still early days in the development of psychotherapy, this book offers some very interesting – and potentially useful – signposts along the way to more effective work in our field.

FOREWORD

Lyman C. Wynne

By the late 1970s, several approaches to family therapy, such as those developed by Minuchin, Whitaker, Bowen, and Boszormenyi-Nagy, had been well explicated and designated (by others) as "schools." As a family therapist who has resisted identification with any "school," I was becoming concerned that the field of family therapy was perhaps following the historical course of psychoanalysis. Both in countless workshops and in many publications, there seemed to be a tendency for followers, if not leaders, to reaffirm factional viewpoints. Repetition and closed circuits, rather than innovation, threatened to characterize the field.

In my view, two centers have provided especially noteworthy exceptions to that trend. One is the well-known Milan group of Selvini-Palazzoli, Cecchin, Boscolo, and Prata. This group, and the two subgroups that have more recently evolved from it, have been widely hailed as providing creative ideas and fresh methods of treatment. A second group, in the less exotic (to Americans) setting of Milwaukee, the Brief Family Therapy Center, deserves to be viewed as an equally creative and generative source of hypotheses and treatment methods. I believe that the present volume by the conceptual leader of the Milwaukee group, Steve de Shazer, should go far to bring proper recognition to the thoughtful originality of this group.

As both this volume and earlier writings illustrate, several features of the approaches developed in Milan and in Milwaukee are remarkably similar although they were mainly developed in parallel rather than through knowledge of each other's current work. Both groups have had an unusual talent for challenging prematurely sanctified beliefs of the family therapy field, for maintaining a self-critical stance, and for a willingness to modify continuously their views in the light of new observations. These qualities have made visits with Steve de Shazer and his colleagues in Milwaukee a true delight because each visit, as well as each new publication, reveals an interesting twist or turn, sometimes in precisely the direction that I least expected. For example, de Shazer has previously described a variety of interesting ways to help families with problem-solving, using methods stimulated by but modified from the late Milton Erickson. Here in the present volume, de Shazer proposes that this emphasis upon problem-solving is based upon a faulty assumption. Instead, he argues that *solutions*, not problems, deserve our primary attention. This shift in focus leads to a conceptually complex conclusion, which has technically simple consequences: The treatment solution does not need to be as complicated as the presenting problem. I shall leave for the reader of this volume the discovery of key ingredients in de Shazer's newest points of entry into therapeutic relationships.

Reading this volume has stimulated me to reflect on the contextual conditions that appear to be shared in Milan and Milwaukee, and that may usefully be considered as other programs organize their activities. Both of these teams have made efforts to develop and maintain genuine dialogue among a small group of colleagues. Role reversals, between therapists and observers, dislodge fixed points of view, but dialogue is protected from excessive intrusion (perhaps facilitated by the difficulty of visiting Milan and Milwaukee). Both groups have deliberately set aside time for making detailed, pinpointed observations of clinical phenomena as well as free-flowing discussions of these observations. Thus, the work has been neither exclusively theoretical nor exclusively method-oriented, but, rather, it has been both/and. This constitutes what I regard as an increasingly and unfortunately neglected form of creative clinical research, namely, disciplined but open-minded exploratory observations not organized by fixed ideology or by research rules. It is probably no accident that neither of these centers is a part of a formal, academic institution, nor do they depend upon approval of external grant support in order to carry out this form of research: explorations spurred on by curiosity about the nature of things. In *clinical* research, this includes curiosity about whether therapy is effective and, especially, about the differences that make a difference.

I commend this volume to readers because they are certain to find at least some matters here with which they can disagree and, thereby, they may be stimulated to reconsider viewpoints that they may have too readily accepted. I feel confident that Steve de Shazer will be among the first to disagree with what he has written and to move forward from the ideas of the present volume. First, readers will want to catch up with where the Milwaukee group is now.

CONTENTS

PREFACE

This book describes a general view of solutions and how they work and of related specific procedures that have been developed during 15 years of doing and studying brief therapy.

In general, when people think about "problems," they tend to follow the lead of the problem-solvers (such as therapists) who think about problems and how they got that way and/or problems and how to solve them. The latter is the approach suggested by Haley (1973) and MRI (Watzlawick, Weakland, and Fisch, 1974), while the former can be represented by most other schools of therapy. However, the idea implicit in both views – that solutions need to have a lot in common with the problem – may be based on a faulty assumption. My work has pointed to the idea (which has been supported by our recent research) that the process of solution, from one case to another, is more similar than the problems each intervention is meant to solve. At first this idea seems counterintuitive, but how else can it be explained that simple formula tasks (that vary little from client to client) promote satisfying change in a wide variety of situations?

A simple metaphor: The complaints that clients bring to therapists are like locks in doors that open onto a more satisfactory life. The clients have tried everything they think is reasonable, right, and good, *and* what they have done was based on their true reality, *but* the door is still locked; therefore, they think their situation is beyond solution. Frequently, this leads to greater and greater efforts to find out why the lock is the way it is or why it does not open. However, it seems clear that solutions are arrived at through keys rather than through locks; and skeleton keys (of various sorts) work in many different kinds of locks. An intervention only needs to *fit* in such a way that the solution evolves. It does not need to match the complexity of the lock. Just because the complaint is complicated does not mean that the solution needs to be as complicated.

In order to readily prompt solutions, it is useful to develop a "vision" or description of a more satisfactory future, which can then become salient to the present. Furthermore, once this "realistic vision" is constructed as one of a set of possible, achievable futures, clients frequently develop "spontaneous" ways of solving the problem. It is the therapist's task, therefore, to develop with the client these expectations of change and solution. In practice, this means that constructing a solution does not need to involve knowing anything about the person's past (unlike traditional therapy), nor does it need to involve knowing, in any detail, what is maintaining the complaint (unlike other types of brief therapy and some types of family therapy). Furthermore, with an open expectation of change, the therapist can promote durable change quite quickly (as our follow-up study indicates).

Unlike most other models of therapy (which assume there is "resistance" between therapist and client), the model described in this book is built on a relationship between therapist and client which is *cooperative* in nature. Since the client comes to therapy wanting change, cooperation can naturally and easily be promoted by the therapist's assumption of an open expectation of change and, therefore, he or she can help to build "visions" of a more satisfactory future. Again, unlike most other models of therapy, this model pays only limited attention to the past, and the little it does is focused almost exclusively on past *successes*. Unlike other models of brief therapy, this model pays relatively little attention to the details of the complaint, focusing instead on *how the client will know when the problem is solved.* Another focal point is on what it is that the clients are doing that is *good* for them, rather than on what is going wrong. These points of emphasis promote the development of a cooperative relationship between therapist and client and are part of the way to find solutions.

This model has been developed in a private, free-standing,

nonprofit, research-and-training-oriented therapy center. Our trainees continue to use and develop the model in various settings including community mental health centers, state and private hospitals, private psychiatric practices, psychological and social work, schools, pastoral counseling, etc. According to our most recent project, "brief" is getting "briefer"; the average number of sessions, per client, was down from six to five.

ACKNOWLEDGMENTS

The Brief Family Therapy Center, which is a research program, has from the beginning been a team effort. As on any team, the various members play vital roles, each necessary to the operation. In many respects, it is a lot like football, where the quarterbacks and halfbacks get all the press while the center, guards, and tackles play vital but essentially unsung roles. It is necessary for the team as a whole to work toward greater coherence and simplicity on both the conceptual and practice levels. These efforts lead to and follow the evidence (i.e., single case examples used as studies as well as larger exploratory projects involving a greater number of cases), supporting the brief therapy tradition of which the research program is but a small part. The whole team is responsible for following up any and all hints which look like they may lead into fruitful areas for investigation and problem-solving. Our business management consultant once remarked that, as far as he could see, the team's purpose was to create and maintain a context in which creativity could happen. As I see it, we are continuing to be successful at that task.

Although I have written this book alone, the ideas cannot help but be influenced by Insoo Berg, Eve Lipchik, Elam Nunnally, and Alex Molnar, who form the core team at this time. As a member of the team, it is difficult for me to see the roles each of us play. What is clear to me is that Insoo and Eve are concerned with the internal connections and implications of our work (i.e., the consistency of the model as a systemic whole), which keeps my concern with simplicity from becoming simplistic or even simple-minded. They are also both quite interested in how a systemic model of brief therapy applies to individual clients. Alex is concerned with the comprehensiveness of our work and the ability to transfer our learning to other contexts. He is also extremely interested in the experimental aspects of practice theory. Elam is concerned with the philosophical and/or epistemological aspects of our work. He is particularly keen on studying how things can go wrong while working within the model and its constraints. Although we all share an interest and concern with training therapists to use the model, the coherence of our approach to training is mainly the result of Insoo's efforts.

Also, newer members of the team, Marilyn Bonjean, Wallace Gingerich, John Walter, and Michele Weiner-Davis, have made contributions to the work described in this book. Marilyn's focus is on working with the elderly, while John's is on training. Wally's particular interest involves bringing more rigor to understanding what it is that the therapist does during the session that is useful in promoting change, and Michele, who focuses mainly on clinical technique, keeps Wally and me from getting too narrow. Jim Derks and Marilyn La Court were members of the team for a time and also contributed to the development of the model.

Any or all of my teammates may disagree with the metaphors I have used in this book, since they might have preferred other metaphors. But these differences are what makes having teams (and subteams) worthwhile. Otherwise, there would be no creativity. Formal discussions, informal discussions (behind the mirror and otherwise), collaboration in workshops and on papers, training other therapists, and drinking beer together – all helped to form the foundations of this book.

In particular, I need to thank Eve Lipchik for what I jokingly call "inserting commas" in the many things I write. Without her skillful editorial help, my articles and this book might well be a maze for the reader.

I also wish to thank our various trainees because helping them learn to do therapy this way forces the whole team to clarify what it is that we do. Without this challenge, our work might not be as well organized.

Outside of the Brief Family Therapy Center world, a special thanks is due to John H. Weakland for his interest and support. His yearly visits help us remain connected to the tradition of which he, his team at the Brief Therapy Center at the Mental Research Institute, and the BFTC team are a part. Over the years we have known each other, he has helped me to clarify what I think is worthwhile in both his model and mine.

Lyman Wynne has indirectly but importantly influenced our work. An offhand comment of his, made when we first met years ago, clarified the whole concept of cooperation for us. He is a true scholar who is able to accept different viewpoints within the larger context of scientific inquiry. Our efforts have benefited from his enjoyable visits.

A special thanks to Susan Barrows of W. W. Norton and Company for her yellow slips, which indicated the care with which she edited the manuscript.

Keys to Solution in
BRIEF THERAPY

1

HOW DO YOU KNOW
WHAT TO DO?

Ever since I began to do and study brief therapy in 1969, the question from observers, "How did you decide to use that particular intervention?" has plagued me. Not only did people ask it of me; I asked it of myself (and other brief therapists). It came up whenever I described or demonstrated my work. The question continues to be asked and answering it, or at least approaching an answer, is the purpose of this book. The first part of this chapter will describe the context or scope of the question and answer. The second section will sketch the evolution of the tradition of which my work is only one part, and the third will describe some of the clues that have led me to my current answer to this question.

BRIEF THERAPY

Time Constraints

Both among professionals and among clients or customers there is a vast amount of confusion about exactly what the term "brief therapy" means. The label suggests that it is distinguished from some other type of therapy which is not brief, i.e., long-term therapy. But what time constraints are there within the limits of "brief" therapy? For some, it is 10 to 25 sessions (Castelnuovo-Tedesco, 1975), whereas for others it can be as many as 40 to 50 sessions (Malan, 1976). Obviously, a tighter definition is needed.

3

Weakland's work at the Brief Therapy Center (Weakland, Fisch, Watzlawick, and Bodin, 1974) of the Mental Research Institute (MRI) was done *within* a 10-session limit. Given that as many as 50 sessions can be considered as "brief," it might be hard to imagine that fewer than 10 sessions can be at all useful, but Weakland et al. reported that 72% of their cases either met their goal for treatment or made significant improvement within an average of seven sessions. Our follow-up study at the Brief Family Therapy Center (using the same questions as those used at MRI) also indicates a 72% satisfaction rate (we didn't state a limit to the number of sessions, but when we were asked, we said, "as few as possible"). This improvement was made within an average of six sessions per client in a randomly selected sample (twenty-five percent of the 1600 cases seen at BFTC from 1978 through 1983). At both settings, phone contact was made with clients between six months and one year after the final therapy session. The person making the contact had not been involved in the therapy.

Fisher (1980, 1984) compared therapy with a six-session limit, therapy with a 12-session limit, and unlimited treatment and found no consistent differences either at termination or at follow-up. A one-year follow-up (Fisher, 1984) provides "no evidence for deterioration in any of the three groups of families that received treatment as part of the original study . . . but there were (statistical) trends for *improvement* from termination to follow-up" (p.104).

Not Just Less of the Same

It is important to define brief therapy other than just in terms of time constraints, because across the board clients tend to stay in therapy from six to ten sessions (Garfield, 1978; Gurman, 1981; Koss, 1979), regardless of the therapist's plans or orientation. If brief therapy were just less of the same, then long-term therapists might be right to "consider it to be a second-rate form of treatment whose effects are merely palliative and temporary" (Fisher, 1984, p. 101). However, Fisher's studies, Weakland's study, and our own study point toward the effectiveness of brief therapy and to the duration of change and additional improvements, rather than the deterioration that could be expected if brief therapy were just a palliative. It has always seemed to me that if the average length of treatment is six to ten sessions, then I (or any other therapist) am ethically compelled to make the most use possible of that limited contact. Since six to ten sessions is all that can be expected, then the model needs to be built on that reality rather than on some ideal, hypothetically unlimited number of sessions. Furthermore, it seems to me that the quicker the problem is solved, the better. The client can get back to living life rather than continuing to suffer through what might be an intractable situation, and the therapist can see more clients when he or she works briefly. That is, I want a distinction between 1) brief therapy (as defined by time constraints), and 2) brief therapy as a way of solving human problems.

EVOLUTION

The published history of brief therapy as presented here can be traced from Milton Erickson's "Special Techniques of Brief Hypnotherapy" (1954a). Erickson's approach seems significantly different from other brief approaches. In this paper he detailed, through seven case examples, an approach that focuses on

> the therapeutic task [which] becomes a problem of intentionally utilizing neurotic symptomatology to meet the unique needs of the patient. Such utilization must satisfy the compelling desire for neurotic handicaps, the limitations imposed upon therapy by external forces, and above all, provide adequately for constructive adjustments aided rather than handicapped by the continuance of neuroticisms. Such utilization is illustrated ... by special hypnotherapeutic techniques of symptom substitution, transformation,

amelioration and the induction of corrective emotional response (in Haley, 1967b, p. 390).

Erickson describes therapy with a 59-year-old man who developed a hysterical paralysis of the right arm. As a result, he faced the joint threat of job loss and pension loss. Erickson told the patient that his was a progressive syndrome which would eventually result in a stiffness in the right wrist while the right arm was in use. As predicted, the paralysis progressed to the point where there was only a stiff wrist, and the man was able to return to work. According to Erickson, in this case and another similar one:

> There was substituted for the existing neurotic disability another, comparable in kind, nonincapacitating in character and symptomatically satisfying to them as constructively functioning personalities. As a result both received that aid and impetus that permitted them to make a good reality adjustment (in Haley, 1967b, p.393).

As I see it, this is the key to brief therapy: *Utilizing what the client brings with him to meet his needs in such a way that the client can make a satisfactory life for himself.* As Erickson put it, no attempt was made to correct any "causative underlying maladjustments" (p.393), and none was needed.

There was then a hiatus during which not much appeared in print about brief therapy. Then, in the late sixties and early seventies, in connection with the growth of family therapy, there were a number of developments. In 1968, the Brief Therapy Center was established at the Mental Research Institute (MRI) in Palo Alto, California; a paper by Weakland, Fisch, Watzlawick, and Bodin, "Brief Therapy: Focused Problem Resolution," was published in 1974; in the same year "The Treatment of Children Through Brief Therapy of Their Parents" (Selvini-Palazzoli, Boscolo, Cecchin, and Prata, 1974) from the Center for the Study of the Family in Milan (begun in 1971) was published; and in 1969 I began to develop a model of brief therapy on my own (without knowledge of the Palo Alto group until 1972), presenting "Brief Therapy: Two's Company" in 1975(a).

These three papers, and two books published during this period — *Change* (Watzlawick, Weakland, and Fisch, 1974) and *Uncommon Therapy* (Haley, 1973) — have much in common: PROBLEMS, how they are maintained, AND HOW TO SOLVE THEM. The focus was clearly on different and effective techniques using a wide variety of cases as illustrations.

One example of my technique around this time (1972) involved telling the parents of a child who messed in his pants

> that six-year-olds like to make messes and really should be allowed mess-making almost as a right. But they, as parents, have a right to select which mess, when, and where. I instructed them to tell the boy that, now that he was six, he was too old to mess his pants, but that he would no longer have to clean up his art mess. In fact, he would not be allowed to (de Shazer, 1975a, p. 87).

CLUES

After 15 years of doing and studying brief therapy, I have come to a conclusion that forms the central premise of this book: For an intervention to successfully *fit*, it is not necessary to have detailed knowledge of the complaint. It is not necessary even to be able to construct with any rigor how the trouble is maintained in order to prompt solution. Given all of my previous work, this at first seemed counter-intuitive, but it does seem that *any* really different behavior in a problematic situation can be enough to prompt solution and give the client the satisfaction he seeks from therapy. All that is necessary is that the person involved in a troublesome situation *does something different*, even if that behavior is seemingly irrational, certainly irrelevant, obviously bizarre, or humorous.

Why Did You Do That?

I continued to work on answering this question, "How does the brief therapist know what to do?" Each intervention seemed tailor-made for the specific client in his specific situation, i.e., for the insomniac who was not reading, staying awake to read proved effective, and for the encopretic, artistic child, making art messes which he did not have to clean up proved effective in stopping pant messes which he did have to clean up. However, the rules behind the interventions were unclear. The only thing certain was that the various cases involved specific behavioral concerns with specific behavioral interventions with a specific goal in mind.

Many of the cases in the articles and books mentioned above seemed to be illustrations of the so-called "symptom prescription" technique, i.e., insomnia cured by staying awake, encopresis by encouraging more messes, homework errors by more mistakes, miscommunication by more miscommunication. However, it was not at all clear how to know what aspect of the "symptom" needed to be prescribed so that a solution would develop. I suspected then that focusing on some other aspects of the troublesome situation might have served to lead to solution as well, while concentration on some other aspects might not have worked at all.

As I saw it at that time,

> the interventions . . . are designed to set up situations in which the family spontaneously behaves differently. They are based on the pattern data the family offers . . . and presented in terms consistent with the family's world view as perceived by the therapist. Although he instructs the client to perform a task, the therapist often has no more idea than the family what specific spontaneous behavior the family may develop in the process of carrying out his instructions . . . The immediate goal is to set up a task that . . . puts the family in a situation in which different behavior is a must (de Shazer, 1975a, p. 84).

The Confusion Technique

In general, brief therapy has tended to focus on clearly defined symptoms, with specific and limited goals. However, I have found that many of my clients (perhaps as many as two-thirds)* do not talk about their concerns in this way, even with my aid – and I much prefer problems that are constructed in concrete and specific terms. The reality is that clients often come with vague and/or mutually exclusive goals or goals which they cannot describe. In fact, the most difficult and confusing version of this is that some people do not know how they will know when their problem is solved. Without realistic goals, without a way to measure success, people can go around in this world mired in the muck of past mistakes and bad luck. This need for goals prompted me to develop a "confusion technique" (de Shazer, 1975b) that I have continued to find useful in helping to construct a problem reality when the clients have extremely vague, mutually exclusive, or even undescribable goals.

Like much of my work in brief therapy, my confusion technique is a development of Erickson's work, in this instance, "The Confusion Technique in Hypnosis" (Erickson, 1964). While Erickson's technique was developed in an experimental setting, he did use it in hypnotherapy with individual patients "desperately seeking therapy but restricted and dominated by their clinical problem" (in Haley, 1967b, p. 151). My technique was designed for use when the confusion was between two or more people with vastly differing reality constructions. While Erickson's technique involves the therapist using highly complex verbal skills and ambiguity in meaning, mine involves exploring in detail each and every possible point of difference between the two people without any attempt at closure or resolution and then openly admitting my confusion in the face of their confusion. In either case, the

---

*Recent research (Chapter 9) indicates that, even in a brief therapy setting, only one-third of the time can the therapist and client construct a specific, concrete problem in the first session.

idea is that the therapist develops rapport and cooperation through utilizing the clients' confusion in such a way that the clients' need to construct meaning in the therapy situation is frustrated and thus the setting of a goal, which gives the situation meaning, is necessitated.

At first I saw the "confusion technique" as simply a way of handling a difficult part of brief therapy that was not dealt with by Haley (1963), or Weakland et al. (1974), or Selvini-Palazzoli et al. (1974): confusion and/or lack of clarity in the construction of the problem(s) and the goal. It's my experience that when doing brief therapy with a couple, it is not unusual for each of the partners to have drastically different ideas about what the "problem" *is* (or even what it might be!), extremely different ideas about who needs to change what, and therefore, radically different or even mutually exclusive ideas about the goals of therapy. I found this to be perhaps more confusing for me than for them. However, once a specific goal is established in these confusing situations, the conditions are set for solutions to develop "spontaneously" in a short period of time. These clearly stated goals do not seem to need to be mutual, just not mutually exclusive; it is, however, necessary that both partners could live with the situation if both their goals were met, or if just one of the goals was met. Of course, the ideal in this situation is to have one agreed-upon goal, and sometimes the couple and I can successfully construct one together.

Although I did not realize it at the time, moving brief therapy out of the limited realm of dealing with neatly defined behavioral complaints and specific behavioral interventions was a radical departure from previous norms. With the two 1975 papers I signaled the beginning of a more comprehensive model of brief therapy, a model that included the therapist's developing problem constructions involving couples and family units in addition to individuals. This has continued to be a major focus of my work and the work of my colleagues at the Brief Family Therapy Center (de Shazer, 1978a, 1982a).

But the question still remained, "How does the brief therapist know what to do, and how to do it?" Or, to put it another way, "How can brief therapy be learned?" With altogether too great a frequency, observers behind the mirror (which I installed in 1971) asked the same question: "Where did *that* intervention come from?" I was puzzled by the question because it seemed obvious to me. I have tried explanation after explanation, metaphor after metaphor, to attempt an answer.

Focus

From 1971 through 1976, I worked on developing a balance-theoretical (Heider, 1946) view of Erickson's principles and procedures.* As a result, I published a series of papers (de Shazer, 1978b, 1979a, 1979b) designed to explicate the rules or guidelines behind Erickson's work and my own. Basically, the central idea was that interventions could be decided upon by using the same map used to describe the way the trouble was being maintained. Balance-theoretical maps, by their rules of construction, suggest a *focus* for intervention by describing the area of the problematic situation most subject to change, which may or may not seem directly related to the "symptom."

These balance-theoretical notions seemed to me to solve some of the issues. However, balance-theoretical maps of couples' and families' relationships are time-consuming and impractical in the everyday world of brief therapy and are, therefore, more suitable for research purposes and *post hoc* explications. Nonetheless, the central idea of mapping the solution on the same map as that used to map the complaint begins to suggest answers about what to do and how to do it.

Indirectness

Indirectness can be seen as one of the identifying fingerprints of brief therapy. Balance-theoretical maps of the client's situation, i.e., the relationship between the client's goal

---

*Jerry Talley and Joseph Berger (both from Stanford University's Sociology Department) were frequent members of the team behind the mirror. After a session, we would trade explanations about what was going on in the therapy room. I taught them about Erickson's principles (as I saw them) and then they would give me a balance-theoretical view (Heider, 1946).

and his or her symptom (de Shazer, 1979a), can be used to point to this central aspect of the approach. "Symptoms" are accepted at face value and, rather than eliminated, transformed into part of the solution. For instance, some years ago a minister came to see me complaining about his having lost God. This, of course, made much of his work difficult for him. He had recently moved to town and was very interested in church architecture. We discussed many of the local landmarks, including churches he had never seen. He thought a friend of his might be interested in adding pictures of these churches to a book, and so – out of this conversation – he went to visit many churches, just to take pictures for his friend. Somewhere along the way, in some church, he again found God. At no time was any formal trance used, nor was it necessary.

Brief hypnotherapy may, or may not, involve a formal induction of a formal trance. Too often, people have a picture of the hypnotist as a magician who "takes over control of the subject." However, as Haley suggests (1958), hypnosis is a term used to describe a certain kind of relationship between people. The term describes a "focused attention" that is part of the interaction between hypnotist and subject: It is not something the hypnotist does to a passive recipient. This view of hypnosis results from Erickson's approach.*

Rather than using traditional trance inductions, Erickson focused on "naturalistic techniques" which can simply arise from the interactional situation. A naïve observer might not know that the brief therapist and the client are using hypnosis because their interaction frequently looks like a more or less normal conversation. The client is not passive, his eyes are not closed, and sleep probably has not even been mentioned. A trained observer would notice therapist and client paying particularly close attention to what the other is saying. He might also notice that therapist and client spontaneously develop metaphors for the topic of conversation which

---

*Haley's edited volume of Erickson's papers (1967b) is still the best book on the subject.

can leave the naïve observer puzzled about what is going on because the terms of the metaphor remain undefined but agreed upon. For instance, I might discuss the process of change with a client in terms of a snowball rolling down a hill and the potential relapse as trees that get in the way of the snowball. However, change and relapse have never been mentioned at all by either party.

It has often seemed curious to me that the brief therapy tradition grew more within the "family therapy" arena than within the "hypnotherapy" arena where it originated. I suspect that the roles Weakland and Haley played in the development of family therapy had a lot to do with it. The brief therapists' view of hypnosis is more compatible with "family therapy" than with much of hypnotherapy because it is based on the interaction between hypnotist and subject (i.e., "systems theory").

In short, brief therapy can be seen as the refinement and development of Erickson's principles for solving clinical problems. These naturalistic, indirect methods are useful with or without formal trances. That is, frequently there is no way for the naïve observer to punctuate his observations so that he can say "there starts a trance induction" or "there starts the trance." All too often, ideas about "trance" and "hypnosis" fascinate the observer and he, therefore, misses the point. Much of the work describing Erickson's work looks too closely at these tools and, thus, by minutely examining the tree's bark, loses sight of the principles involved in the whole forest. The interest in Erickson's techniques of hypnosis clouds over his uses of hypnosis. Hypnosis is more like novocaine than it is like tooth extraction. By itself, novocaine is rather useless and teeth can be extracted without it.

If It Works, Don't Fix It

I continued to look for a satisfactory explication (or set of explanations) of Erickson's work which I saw as guiding mine (and MRI's). Once more I turned to balance theory to explore how the symptomatic behavior can be seen as exactly that which is preventing achievement of the client's goal (de Shazer, 1979a). It was clear to me that the goal of therapy is not "elimination of the symptom" but, rather, helping the client set up some conditions that allow for the spontaneous achievement of the stated (or inferred) goal. In most cases, a new and beneficial meaning can be constructed for at least some aspect of the so-called symptom. It is not *either* a person has a symptom *or* he does not. That a certain behavior is labeled a symptom is arbitrary: In some other setting or with a different meaning attached, the same behavior would be both appropriate and normal.

For instance, in 1973, I treated a young woman who wanted to get married to her boyfriend but found herself silenced by undefined and undefinable fears, not only with him but also increasingly in other social situations. She wanted to stop being silent. As part of the intervention message at the end of the session, I congratulated her

> on having mastered the hardest part of communication skills: how to keep silent and listen. What she had to learn next was much, much easier. She had to learn when other people were really ready to listen. Therefore, she was given the assignment to go home and listen to her boyfriend when he talked to her and other people. She was not to attempt to talk any more than usual, perhaps less. Rather, she was to study and learn the signals he sent when and if he was really ready and willing to listen. Subsequent sessions concerned what she learned. She was given further directives to watch other talkers in other situations, but not to start joining conversations until she was sure she knew the signals (de Shazer, 1979a, p. 25–26).

That is, the task of deliberately keeping silent to learn signals (rather than keeping silent because of fear) was constructed so that she would create the conditions in which she could "spontaneously" begin talking. Importantly, the silence was not eliminated; rather, it was just transformed into something of value. Once she was comfortable talking, she could approach her boyfriend with the idea of getting married – an idea that was agreeable to him. Also, she could remain silent when she wanted to.

Death of Resistance

By 1979 a new perspective was developing. I had long been puzzled by the notion of "resistance" in therapy. As I watched other brief therapists* work, I became more and more convinced that clients really do want to change. Certainly some of them found that the ideas about *how* to change did not fit very well. However, I found it difficult to label this as "resistance" when it seemed to be a message the clients were sending in an effort to help the therapist help them (de Shazer, 1979c). Over and over I found people sent to me by other therapists (complete with the label "resistant client") to be both desperate for change and highly cooperative. Actually, the key my colleagues and I invented for promoting cooperation is quite simple.

> *First we connect the present to the future (ignoring the past), then we compliment the clients on what they are already doing that is useful and/or good for them, and then – once they know we are on their side – we can make a suggestion for something new that they might do which is, or at least might be, good for them.*

Frequently people nod and smile and obviously relax during and after this kind of message.

---

*Insoo Berg, Elam Nunnally, Eve Lipchik, and Alex Molnar are the core members of the team at the Brief Family Therapy Center which was begun in 1978. More recently, Marilyn Bonjean, Wallace Gingerich, John Walter, and Michele Weiner-Davis have joined the group. Jim Wilk has joined the group subsequent to the work described here. For a time, Jim Derks and Marilyn La Court were part of the group. Unless otherwise noted, the therapist in the various cases described in this book was one of the members of this group.

I have often been rather surprised by what clients say has happened to them since our previous meeting. Sometimes they have revised the suggestion so that it fits better for them, and the problem is clearly headed toward solution. Sometimes they thought the suggestion was simply wrong and, reasonably, decided not to use it. Nonetheless, things had become better for them or even, on not so rare occasions, the problem was headed toward solution and they were more satisfied. Although not doing an assigned task or drastically changing an assigned task is frequently seen or described by therapists as "resistance," my colleagues and I have a difficult time constructing reality in such a way.

Clearly, people come to therapy wanting to change their situation. But whatever they have done to attempt change has not worked. They have been getting in their own way, perhaps have accidentally made their own situation worse, and have developed unfortunate habit patterns. Given this, the idea that they are going to resist change is at least misguided. In fact, with this kind of idea in mind, the therapist can actually generate "resistance" (Fisch, Weakland, and Segal, 1983) or noncooperation, if not conflict. That is, the therapist's notions could generate a self-fulfilling prophecy with an unsuccessful outcome.

Only a Small Change Is Needed

I have found the idea that only a small change is necessary, and therefore only a small and reasonable goal is necessary, makes it far easier to develop a cooperative relationship between therapist and client. One major difference between brief therapy and other models lies in the brief therapist's idea that no matter how awful and how complex the situation, a small change in one person's behavior can make profound and far-reaching differences in the behavior of all persons involved.* Both clinical experience and research seem to con-

---

*John Weakland and I have frequently discussed this point of view which brief therapists (at MRI and at BFTC) seem to hold quite strongly. I think that this expression of the idea uses his words.

firm the idea that a small change can lead to other changes and, therefore, further improvement. Furthermore, it seems that the bigger the goal or the desired change, the more likely therapist and client will fail.

Since brief therapy is based on systems theory, I have been puzzled for a long time by the idea some therapists have that "family therapy" means that the therapist *must* meet with the whole family or that "couples therapy" demands that both spouses be present. Their idea seems to be that systems theory, which posits that the whole is greater than the sum of the parts, dictates the necessity of having the whole family unit in therapy. All along, this restricted view has led me to reject the label "family therapist" for myself, even though systems theory is one of my map-making tools. If the client is one person, certain methods and techniques are useful in finding solutions. If the "client" is two, or three, or more people, then the same methods and a different group of methods and techniques are useful. To paraphrase Gertrude Stein: A solution is a solution is a solution. Since only a small change is necessary to initiate change in a system, the number of people who are in on successfully constructing the problem and the solution does not matter. For brief therapists their "patient" is the problem: This is the essential difference between brief therapy and other therapies for whom the "patient" is a person or persons.

2

COMPLAINTS: DAMN BAD LUCK

WORKING WITH A TEAM: STIMULATING BUT NOT NECESSARY

The first phase of my work involved teaching myself how to do brief therapy with the aid of Erickson's work (Haley, 1967b) and Haley's (1963), and the second phase involved working in front of a one-way mirror with observers behind. Before and after the session we would talk about the therapy, but during the session they had their job while I had mine. In 1976, I discovered a group of like-minded therapists in Milwaukee who eventually founded the Brief Family Therapy Center with me in 1978. For the first time the people behind the mirror did not ask, "How come you did that?" Rather, they wondered about how we might teach people how to work effectively and research this way of working.

Although our philosophies and clinical methods were quite similar, those of us who founded BFTC did have some differences in our language. I was influenced more by the work of Milton Erickson than they were, while they were more influenced by family therapy. In order to pragmatically settle our language differences, we developed a team approach using a regularly scheduled intra-session break to consult with each other about the design of the intervention, which one of us would deliver upon returning to the therapy room. Prior to our agreement on this procedure, I sometimes took a break to hurriedly consult *Advanced Techniques* (Haley, 1967b) for a hint, or to get help from behind the mirror when I felt too stuck. Quite unknown to us, the Milan group had developed a similar format (Selvini-Palazzoli, Boscolo, Cecchin, and Prata, 1978).

Behind the mirror, we developed maps about the complaints: behavior and meaning or context, the goals, and the potential areas for initiating change. The interventions that we used were structured in such a way that cooperation between client and therapist was promoted. *Patterns of Brief Family Therapy* (de Shazer, 1982a) describes this phase, during which the team members behind the mirror became more and more active participants in the doing of the therapy. Although working solo was briefly described, the focus was clearly on the team's approach to clinical research, practice, and model-building. This, perhaps, promoted the mistaken idea that a team is necessary for "working this way." The team's usefulness lies in research, experimentation, teaching, training, model-building, but, alas, it is not a practical approach for most therapists to use in doing therapy. A team is not *necessary* for working this way. Useful, certainly! Stimulating, certainly!

When several therapists observe the same case from behind a mirror, each one contributes his or her own knowledge about troublesome situations and the knowledge of solutions based on previous results. One might read the "data" as an example of Situation A, while another might see it as Situation B, and yet a third might map it as Situation R. If the experience is a busman's holiday, then A, B, and R can be taken as just a set of maps with interesting differences. Competition, should it arise, might well be friendly and humorous. However, when observing a case together becomes an ongoing situation that the group wants to continue, then a foundation of cooperation is necessary for the development of a team.

The Poly-ocular View

Bateson (1979) described ideas as developing from having two or more descriptions of the same process, pattern, system, or sequence that are coded or collected differently. A

bonus – the idea – develops out of the differences between or
among descriptions. Metaphorically, this process is similar
to that of depth perception. The right eye sees things in its
way, while simultaneously the left eye sees things differently.
The difference between the two eyes' views leads to the bonus
of depth perception. Clearly, it is not that the right eye is correct while the left eye is wrong or vice versa.

When a group of therapists is behind the mirror, each
codes or collects the information differently. It is not just a
matter of selecting what to note from a heap of available information. Rather, the therapist's model, which includes a set
of assumptions, determines how the therapist will construct
or interpret what he or she has seen. Each therapist in the
group sees something different and, at least metaphorically,
a bonus develops which gives the group more depth or ideas.
Importantly, there is no sense in which one therapist's construction is "right" while the others' ideas are "wrong." Their
views are just different; these differences are useful and
prompt creativity.

The Development of a Team

Axelrod's work (1984) confirms our experience that, when
the future of the group is important to the group, then cooperation will evolve and thus the group will become a team.
Of course, each member of the team must have a high level
of trust and confidence in the other members' ability; otherwise the team will degenerate into factionalism and competition and be ineffective. Early on, the BFTC team had members from various "schools" and it was necessary to dampen
the factionalism so that the work could be facilitated. We
discovered that our productivity and creativity increased
as we continued to work together and, as Ouchi (1981) suggests, a culture developed based on the philosophy of the
team.

We took several steps to facilitate the development of the

team. First, we made a conscious decision to isolate ourselves from other groups of family therapists once we became a "free-standing" center. This allowed us to have the freedom to be creative in our therapy. Secondly, we each redesigned our interviewing techniques. Primarily, this meant a process of simplification, eliminating much of what was idiosyncratic to the various schools, i.e., one gave up doing "enactments" while another gave up doing "sculpting" and we all gave up "instant relabeling." Although individual variations continued, we developed a consistency of interviewing techniques which makes the tasks behind the mirror easier to perform.

Our purpose in using the team was never to develop a team approach to therapy. Rather, we wanted to find out as much as we could about what we did that was effective. Fortunately, we all agreed that reported and/or observed changes in behavior within the complaint pattern and the end of the complaint (i.e., the "symptoms" stopped) were good enough indicators of success. This, of course, necessitated follow-up contacts, which have been routine from the start. In addition, we studied the short-range effects of our interventions. At the end of a session, we generally gave some sort of homework. Frequently this included a behavioral task which was checked on as the first order of business in the following session.

We quickly found that the rate of task performance was higher than it had seemed prior to the development of the team and the new procedures (de Shazer, 1982a). We also found that we could get as much information when the client did not perform the task as when the client did perform the task. Not only that, we also found that accepting nonperformance as a message about the clients' way of doing things (rather than as a sign of "resistance") allowed us to develop a cooperating relationship with clients which might not include task assignments. This was a shock to us because we had assumed that tasks were almost always necessary to achieve behavioral change. Thus, we became more successful with more clients in a fewer number of sessions.

COMPLAINTS AND HOW THEY GET THAT WAY

Therapists need to make some assumptions about the construction of complaints and the nature of solutions in order to do their job. Although the following set of assumptions is somewhat idiosyncratic, nonetheless there is a fairly high degree of similarity with Watzlawick et al. (1974) and with Haley (1963, 1973). Some aspects of the following assumptions about complaint construction lead inevitably to ways of constructing solutions. Problem-solving has been studied experimentally (see Mayer, 1983, for an overview), and this work can be suggestive about the nature of complaints and about the "unconstruction" of problems.

These assumptions can be seen to operate like the rules for mapping complaints and problems. If a therapist uses a certain set of assumptions, say "Y," then a certain type of map will develop. Let's say that the therapist assumes that symptoms have a systemic function, i.e., holding the family together. In this case he will attempt to draw a map which suggests to him how that function can be served in that system without the symptom. However, if the therapist uses set "X," a different type of map will develop. For instance, the therapist might assume that a symptom is just a matter of "bad luck" and does not serve a function; therefore, he will draw a different map that suggests eliminating the symptom by substituting what might have happened if there had been some "good luck."

Although the following assumptions seem central and basic, there are probably others (on some "deeper" levels) underlying the practice of brief family therapy. Although all the assumptions work together to influence practice, some individually have the "power" or "strength" to directly influence or even prescribe specific therapeutic interventions, while others have the "power" to directly inform the therapist about how to construct a problem in such a way that solutions develop. In certain situations, one particular assumption might seem more directly influential, while in other situations the interaction between two or more assumptions can be seen more clearly. A hypothetical model of complaints will be in-

terwoven with the descriptions of our assumptions so that
reasoning behind the assumptions is clarified.

Assumption One

*Complaints involve behavior brought about by the cli-
ent's world view.*

The first step in building a complaint seems relatively
small, although the consequences can be rather dispropor-
tionate. It is as if people say, "I either behave in 'A' fashion
or I believe in 'non-A' fashion. For whatever reason (or set of
reasons), 'A' seems to be the right (logical, best, or only)
choice." As a result, everything else (all "non-A") is lumped
together and excluded. That is, the "either" behavior ("A")
seems as though it is in a class by itself, and the "or" behaviors ("non-A") seem to be all the remaining classes (all classes
minus Class "A") of behavior that might have been chosen.
Hypothetically, a complaint can be constructed out of just
about anything or even nothing (Watzlawick, 1983), somewhat in the following (undoubtedly oversimplified) manner.

A Model of Complaints, Part One

Bed-wetting is a behavior that is relatively common and
rather normal for children, which, under various conditions,
can easily become a complaint. When a child wets the bed,
the parent makes a decision every time (1) about how to view
this behavior: (a) normal behavior or (b) problematic behavior.
If the decision is that it is normal, then things go on, "one
damn thing after another." However, if decision (1b) is made,
the following tree develops. Decision (1b) requires decision (2):
that the bed-wetting is (a) a physical problem or (b) a psychological problem. If the decision is that the child has a physical
problem (2a), the next step is relatively obvious, although
physical intervention may not prove to be helpful. If (2b) is
the choice, the child with a psychological problem can be seen
as (3) either (a) bad or (b) mad.

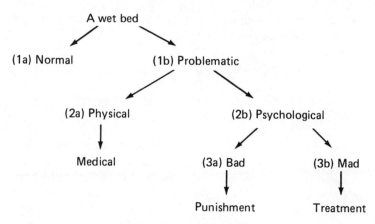

Figure 2.1   Complaint Tree

In the event that the parent decides that the child's problem is psychological (2b), the next step is not so clear. If the child is seen as "bad" (3a), then various punishments might be applied in the effort to stop the bad behavior. If the child is seen as "mad" (3b), then any treatment, professional or not, might be tried. Of course, the situation often is not this simple.

At any decision point (1, 2, or 3), a child with two parents might have one parent picking "a" and the other picking "b," and some parents might not be able to choose between "a" and "b." In this way the child's bed-wetting can be seen as if "coming between the parents," which is a map used by many therapists and thus an even bigger problem (4) can evolve: either (a) mother is right or (b) father is right. In some families, if one parent "wins," the whole tree (1, 2, and 3) might be gone through; then, if the "winner" is proved wrong, the other parent might take a turn at trying to solve the complaint. Even in-laws might get involved in defining the situation, potentially adding chaos to confusion.

Another possible branching (5) occurs when the question arises, "Who is to blame for the problem?" It might be (a) the child's fault or (b) the parents' fault. If there are two parents, it can be either (a) mother's fault or (b) father's fault. Complaints can be constructed in various ways depending upon who is at fault, or how the complaint is framed.

Assumption Two

Complaints are maintained by the clients' idea that what they decided to do about the original difficulty was the only right and logical thing to do. Therefore, clients behave as if trapped into doing more of the same (Watzlawick et al., 1974) because of the rejected and forbidden half of the either/or premise.

When driving we reach many decision points, "Should I turn right or should I turn left?" If one turns right, everything on the route to the left remains unsampled and unexperienced. In an interactive system such as a family, essentially similar decision points can occur over and over ("The

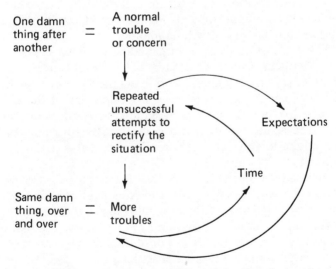

Figure 2.2 The Process of Complaint Development

bed is wet again."). However, once the "right" decision has been reached, the response to the wet bed becomes as habitual as the wet bed. People do not stop to remake the decision and see each wet bed as distinct. Rather, they see it as, "Here we go again." Brief therapists call this, "The same damn thing over and over."

A Model of Complaints, Part Two

Once the "right" decision is made (e.g., bed-wetting is a problem), then people set about trying to solve it. For instance, if the child is framed as willfully wetting (bad), then the child needs to be punished. Punishment can take many forms, and it seems to escalate when it does not work. First one punishment is tried, then either more of the same punishment or an (apparently) different punishment (which is logically more of the same) is tried. Wet beds continue to follow punishments, while punishments continue to follow wet beds in a "never ending" round of frustration and perhaps anger. Since the initial decision was the only "right" one, "the same damn thing over and over" is perfectly logical: There must be an "effective" punishment. People seem to think that as long as they persist, it will be found!

The cycle of punishment/wet bed/punishment continues with each step escalating in turn, but the decision "this is a behavior that needs punishment" is frequently not called into question. On the "either/or" tree, the relabeling of the child as "mad" or "normal" has been excluded by the decision and, therefore, so have all the many possible different things parents might do which are not (logically identical with the) punishments.

Once this "either/or" construction is recognized, it follows that *any* "non-A" behavior might make enough of a difference (by lifting people out of their rigidity) to provide a solution. In this sense, "either/or" thinking can be seen as the root of many clients' complaints. This line of thinking involves standard binary logic, and systemic situations do not seem to operate according to the rules of binary logic (Wilden, 1980).

Therefore, "systemic or cybernetic logic" is called for, i.e., what Bateson (1979) calls the "twin stochastic process" or, more simply, randomness.

RECONSTRUCTING COMPLAINTS INTO PROBLEMS

As we have continued to work together, our interviewing style has continued to simplify as we developed a poly-ocular view of the situation: Each therapist maps the same situation differently (but not competitively). In our opinion, the multiple maps enhance and enrich the possibility of change. Clients' complaints are usually rather complex constructions involving many elements, any one of which they may emphasize more than the others. We have learned that complaints generally include:

1. a bit or sequence of behavior;
2. the meanings ascribed to the situation;
3. the frequency with which the complaint happens;
4. the physical location in which the complaint happens;
5. the degree to which the complaint is involuntary;
6. significant others involved in the complaint directly or indirectly;
7. the question of who or what is to blame;
8. environmental factors such as jobs, economic status, living space, etc.;
9. the physiological or feeling state involved;
10. the past;
11. dire predictions of the future; and
12. utopian expectations.

If there are two or more people talking to the therapist, they may agree or disagree about the definition, importance, and significance of any of the elements. Fortunately, couples and families are micro-cultures; therefore, the elements deemed important often overlap and each element is somehow connected to one or more of the other elements.

Each of these elements seems to be connected to all of the other elements in the complaint construction in such a way that they define each other. Consequently, a change in one can "lead to" changes in the others. The same event will be defined in various ways due to the various other factors involved in the situation. For instance, we all know that if the car does not start, our reaction will differ according to how we feel. If we are already "down," the stalled car will be just one more thing going wrong. But if we are "on top of the world," then the stalled car will be nothing more than a minor inconvenience. From situation to situation, some elements may be more connected or more pertinent than others. For example, frequently clients complain of feeling (usually phrased as "being") depressed. Some will immediately be able to describe the behavioral aspects of it, while others find that difficult or impossible; therefore, they will focus on the involuntary aspects. Some will easily describe significant others who are trying to cheer them up (accidentally making it worse), while others find that difficult and instead bemoan the fact that historically they have good reasons to be depressed. Still others are depressed about something they are sure is going to happen (or not happen) in the future.

During the interview, the therapist asks questions about each of the areas listed above and illustrated in Figure 2.3, attempting to define the problem in such a way that a solution can develop. Each client seems to have "favorite" factor(s) that he or she chooses to emphasize in the description of the problem. Likewise, the therapists behind the mirror map the information in ways which they deem important (using similar categories). Our collective experience since 1977 indicates that any of the 12 factors can be subject to change, and the change of one factor can be followed by changes in the others.

Although there is no one-to-one relationship between the building blocks used to construct complaints and those used to construct interventions, nonetheless what clients emphasize strongly suggests possibilities. For instance, if the complaint is described as happening only in one particular place,

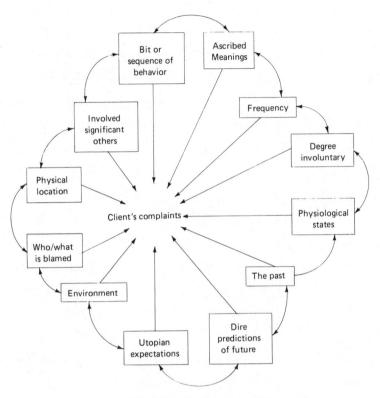

Figure 2.3 The Building Blocks of Complaints

then task assignments – particularly anything directly to do with the complaint behaviors themselves – need to be scheduled to happen in some other location in order to assure some minimal difference. For example, couples sometimes report that their fights happen only in the kitchen. Many behaviors seem to be situationally specific and the therapist can simply prescribe that the next fight occur in the bedroom. There is a good chance that the different "stage" will prompt different behavior. They might make up with a good sexual experience. Or, if the complaint involves a relationship to some person not

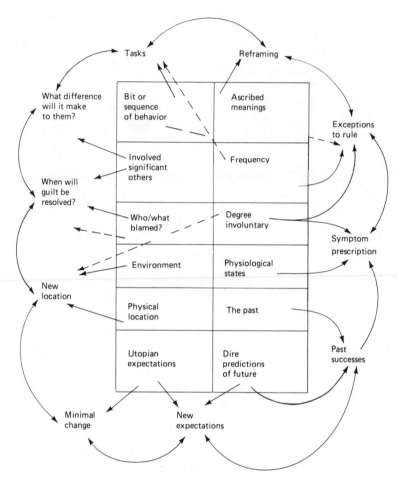

Figure 2.4 Transforming Complaints Toward Solution

in the therapy room, then a major question revolves around
how the other person(s) will know that a change has occurred.

A Metaphor

These 12 factors are like 12 different doors leading to solutions. Each complaint is different, and the various potential

solutions are the doors that have the better oiled locks and hinges. Various doors may lead to the same solutions or different solutions, while the same door may lead to different solutions. Any door may lead to a blind alley. Together, therapist and client have to figure out which door is the most likely to be the easiest to open. Since they are all locked with different locks, needing different keys (otherwise the client would have found his way out), a skeleton key would be useful.

Behind the mirror, each team member maps the client's presentation in a different way. If the team is large enough or experienced enough, any door and each of the doors might play an important role in the maps drawn by an individual therapist. For instance, a behaviorist probably would want to use the behavioral door to the solution but, for any given client, this door might be really stuck and, therefore, therapy might fail. However, when there is a team behind the mirror, the behaviorist might learn that other doors might be easier to open. If there is a team of three and one client, then there are at least four different realities made out of this material and we have a poly-ocular view.

Importantly, it is not that the team members just see things from different angles or perspectives. Rather, they each construct a different therapeutic reality based on the information provided by the client during the interview. One member of the team may map the situation by focusing on the client's complaint as related to another person, while another may map the information in such a way that the client's reaction to feeling states is emphasized, and another may emphasize the client's perception of the involuntary nature of the complaint. Each of these separately points to particular potential solutions. As the team discusses the problem construction, a different approach is often noticed. For instance, with this combination of individual views, the team might develop the idea that the most potential for change lies in the differences of location—where the complaint happens and where it does not.

Each client constructs the complaint reality out of these 12 factors, and each therapist constructs the therapeutic reality (complaint plus potential solutions) out of the same materials, but with a focus on solution. Because of the different emphases in the therapists' constructions, the therapeutic problem will be "different" from the complaint construction. It is this difference which leads to solution.

As the therapeutic reality is constructed, the question about which door is most likely to be useful looms large. This can sometimes prove troublesome when the client's least favorite door (i.e., behavior change) is the one the therapists think will most easily lead to solutions. So, the therapist needs to find out which are the favored doors, the best indicator for that being *how* the client describes the complaint. For example, if the client is complaining about feeling depressed because of his past (and, therefore, he cannot help himself), then behavioral tasks might be the least likely entry, even though they might be the easiest for the therapist to devise and might lead to the quickest solutions. In this case, the client's description and his language (Watzlawick et al., 1974) suggest that the depression is involuntary and that he blames it on his past actions or on others. Two types of keys (therapeutic interventions) might prove useful in this case. One is called a "symptom prescription" in which the therapist suggests that the client force himself to be more depressed (the "involuntary" door) in order to become less depressed. The other key, "reframing," would involve ascribing different frames or meanings to the depression in such a way that the client will find it beginning to make more sense to not be depressed (the "ascribed meanings" door). (The distinction between these two keys is not always clear-cut, pointing to the skeleton key aspect of at least some interventions.) Although these keys might work well, the locks and hinges might be rusty and, therefore, solutions might be slow in developing. Which door to use? Which key will be useful?

In many cases, this locked room mystery is approached by the therapist's gathering as much information as possible about the 12 elements or about what it is that keeps the client stuck in the complaint. Reasonably, therapists (and other troubleshooters) often think that more information will be useful, which it is in some situations. However, somewhere along the line more information can cross a barrier and usefulness can turn to confusion. In order to find a solution, the question is not, "How much information is needed?" but rather, "What kind of information is needed?"

THE CONSTRUCTION OF SOLUTIONS

Assumption Three

> *Minimal changes are needed to initiate solving complaints and, once the change is initiated (the therapists' task), further changes will be generated by the client (the "ripple effect" [Spiegel and Linn, 1969]).*

The way change develops is similar to the way a small error can end up making a big difference. If a pilot upon leaving New York for San Francisco makes a one degree error in direction, when he should be in San Francisco he will instead be considerably off course.

A simple rule might be proposed here: Clients frequently present their complaint in either/or terms and, in these situations, it can be useful for the therapist to construct the problem in both/and terms. The switch from either/or to both/and is useful on the law-schema and map-making levels and, as a heuristic, on the action-schema level. The clinical techniques follow not only from successful practice but also from the more philosophical and conceptual work on "systems" (Wilden, 1980).

A Model of Complaints, Part Three

If the parent(s) of the bed wetter are to solve this, they need to break the repeating cycle. However, anything other than punishments has been excluded by the earlier decisions. It is exactly these excluded and forbidden responses which stand a chance of solving the problem (stopping both the parental approach and the wet beds). For instance, rewarding dry beds, or ignoring wet beds, or teaching the child to wash his wet bedding, or hanging up a sign in the child's room which says, "Wet The Bed Tonight"—all have worked in some situations. The point is that *any* new behavior stands a chance of being different enough, and *all* these have been forbidden by the "same damn thing" rule after the "right" decision was made.

In choosing a new response, we find it useful to look for exceptions to the rule. It seems overly simple-minded to say that nothing is ever exactly like anything else. If the child's bed was wet last night, the night before, and the night before, etc.—which causes people to say "the child always wets the bed"—the bed might be more wet on one night than on the next, or more dry. And the child might have wet the bed at a different time on different days and probably the sheets are different. Although the child is seen as always wetting the bed, there are probably some dry nights now and then— *exceptions to the rule* (an important concept developed jointly by the author, Wallace Gingerich and Michele Weiner-Davis to describe what the therapist is after during the first session). However, these exceptions frequently slip by unnoticed because these differences are not seen as differences that make any difference: The difference is too small or too slow.

These exceptions to the rules of the pattern are exactly the kind of information the therapist needs to know. It is important for the therapist, the child, and the parent(s) to know that the child in some (perhaps unconscious?) way knows how to have a dry bed! And, therefore, there are times when a dry bed pattern operates in this family. The therapist needs to find out: What are the differences between the dry bed pattern and the wet bed pattern? Then he can figure out how the dry bed pattern can be used to form the basis of an intervention that solves the problem. What differences does the child's having a dry bed make to the rest of the family? What change is there in the parents' attitude toward the child?

Of course, any intervention into a wet bed pattern based on the family's dry bed exceptions to that pattern will have the benefit of *fitting*, since it is part of the family's reality (it is, after all, their solution). This can only promote cooperation and increase the chances of problem solution.

Case Example: Toward Being a Perfect Mother*

Mrs. Baker came to therapy complaining about her approach to her children. She thought she should *completely* stop yelling at them because the yelling did not achieve its aim and just left her frustrated. Trying to establish a minimal goal, the therapist asked her, "What sort of thing do you think will happen when you start to, Joan take a more calm and reasonable approach to your children?"** The phrasing recasts the goal as the start of something (a more calm and reasonable approach), rather than Mrs. Baker's impossible goal of stopping yelling completely. This start then can be measured and known by Mrs. Baker. It could be something very small indeed that occurs in between yellings that would allow the yellings to happen now and then without their necessarily being seen as a setback. In fact, the therapist directed Mrs. Baker to randomly decide, by a toss of the coin, between (1) yelling and (2) a calm approach, and to figure out, based on the results, when to do which. She reported discovering that sometimes yelling was the best thing to do, and sometimes a calm and reasonable approach was more effective.

With a question structured in this way, the therapist not

---

*For security and confidentiality reasons we give titles to cases, particularly to those we videotape. These titles sometimes are relevant, sometimes not.

**This kind of unusual sentence structure will be found throughout in the verbatim excerpts from intervention messages and therapist's questions during the session: "What sort of thing do you think *will* happen *when* you start to, Joan take a more calm and reasonable approach to your children?" Several messages are implicit here: (1) the idea or suggestion that Joan should take a more calm and reasonable approach (the second part after the comma), (2) the expectation that Joan will take this approach (the "when" before the comma, not an "if"), and (3) the expectation that a more calm and reasonable approach will make a difference that Joan can notice (things will happen). This structure is derived from the hypnotic techniques developed by Milton Erickson (Haley, 1967b; Erickson, Rossi, and Rossi, 1976; Erickson and Rossi, 1979). It is our view that brief therapy sessions employ hypnotic techniques whether or not a formal trance is used (see Chapter 5). Therefore, we tend to follow Erickson's lead in the construction and use of therapeutic suggestions.

only recasts the goal as the start of something, but also makes the goal achievement into a therapeutic suggestion. This allows the client to view the change as self-generated, minimizing the therapeutic interference.

When Mrs. Baker came for therapy she framed the complaint as *either* she yelled all the time *or* she stopped yelling entirely. She had tried to stop yelling, but these efforts were not successful and only led to more frustration. However, the expectation she had that she should and could completely stop yelling is unrealistic. There are times when any mother of small children is going to yell at her children, and there may be times when yelling is the best thing to do. The therapeutic suggestion that she randomly start taking a more calm and reasonable approach recast her problematic either/or frame into a both/and frame. Mrs. Baker can *both* take a calm and reasonable approach *and* she can yell. The decision is hers to make, and hopefully she will develop some decision-making procedures other than the coin toss.

There is a bonus to this approach. Mrs. Baker reported a ripple effect resulting from her different behavior. Once Mrs. Baker randomized her approach, the children no longer found her so predictable and, therefore, the "causes" of mother's yelling diminished both in frequency and intensity. In a matter of three weeks, the yelling took on a new meaning: Mother means business since she is not being calm and reasonable. This approach to solving Mrs. Baker's problem allowed her a high degree of freedom in her response to the interventions. Both yelling and not yelling are acceptable responses. Of course, not yelling includes a lot of behaviors which can be framed as "starting to take a more calm and reasonable approach." Even deciding *once* to not yell when she thought she normally would have yelled would be a minimal change that could lead to solution of the problem.

This approach fully accepts Mrs. Baker as she presents herself (a yeller), does not scold her for it, does not tell her to change by eliminating the yelling, and would not consider any continued yelling as a sign of resistance; it is a *cooperating* mode of therapy.

Case Example: The Key

A mother brought her two children (a daughter, age 15, and a son, nine) to therapy because the girl, who had been an honor roll student in the past, was on her way to setting a record for number of days absent from school. Each morning, mother would tell the girl to go to school and the daughter would say that she was going and she would leave home at the proper time. Then, as soon as mother went to work, the girl would come back home and watch TV all day. Since mother spent a lot of time talking about the girl's past achievements, the therapist became interested in mother's past successes. At one point the mother had taken the girl's keys away and the girl went to school. However, mother was concerned about the safety of both children after school until she returned from work. Therefore, she gave the keys back.

Since taking the keys had worked before, the team thought that this was the simplest intervention possible. Mother had explained her reasoning and the team was afraid she would not follow through if they told her to take the keys away. Therefore, the team constructed the following message:

> "We don't know when, Marsha is going to go back to school and stay there, and we don't know if you, mother, know when, Marsha is going back to school, and we don't know if you, Sam, know when, Marsha is going back to school, and we don't know if you, Marsha, know when you are going back to school. We don't know *who holds* the *key* to this problem."*

On the way home from the session, mother took Marsha's keys and the next day arranged for a neighbor to supervise Sam after school. Marsha returned to school and, as reported two weeks later, continued to attend. By not directly telling mother to take the girl's keys, the team was able to allow mother to save face and to have the idea herself. The indirect

*Intervention messages quoted in this book are as close to verbatim as possible.

method allowed, therefore, for the minimal intervention possible. The follow-up reports again indicate that the ripple effect occurred: Marsha went to school, stayed in school once there, and resumed getting good grades.

Assumption Four

> *Ideas about what to change are based on ideas about what the clients' view of reality might be like without the particular complaint.*

During the interview, both in front of the mirror and behind, we try to build scenarios about how the client's situation will be different *after* the therapeutic goal has been achieved. If, for instance, a dry bed would not seem to make any real difference in how the boy and his parents relate to each other, then perhaps how the parents view the child and how the child views the parents should be the focus of the therapeutic efforts. If this hypothetical solution seems to include dry beds, then the "ascribed meaning" door, or the "blame" door, or the "environment" door might be more useful than some other doors.

A Model of Complaints, Part Four

Most simply, if the parents think of the wet bed as only one of the many signs that mean "this is a bad kid," then just initiating dry beds is not likely to shift their framing of the situation in such a way that it can be the solution. The therapist needs to at least create some doubt about the meaning of the wet bed and/or create some doubt about the frame "this is a bad child." Frequently, some doubt can be created by the therapist's describing wet beds as a normal problem given other circumstances of the child's life, i.e., whenever an overly sensitive and creative child is mistaken for a bad child, bedwetting will continue until the child is convinced that he will continue to receive just as much attention when he has a dry bed and/or until the parents are able to convince him that he will receive just as much attention when he has a dry bed. (A child who is always doing things that cause trouble can frequently be effectively labeled as "creative" and the bed-wetting proves his sensitivity.) Of course, a dry bed following this sort of framing needs to be viewed with the utmost caution: The family needs to be warned that the child might create some more trouble until he is really convinced!

Regardless of the specific situation, the therapist needs to know what meaning(s) the client ascribes to the complaint. Frequently meaning(s) can be found by asking about what the client thinks things will be like when the problem is solved. What a "wet bed" means or what a "dry bed" means helps to determine the frame the therapist can use to effectively solve the problem. For the "bad kid," a dry bed is not enough. The child will probably be seen as doing something else equally "bad." Once the therapist knows these negative meanings (frames), he can reframe by substituting positive meanings for the same behaviors (de Shazer, 1982a).

Assumption Five

A new frame or new frames need only be suggested, and new behavior based on any new frame can promote clients' resolution of the problem.

An Experimental Approach to the Construction of Frames

Duncker (1945) designed the following experiment which illustrates how frames (definitions and meanings) influence what happens. Group One was given three boxes, one with matches, one with candles, and one with tacks. Group Two received the same materials, but the matches, candles and tacks were not *in* the boxes. The object was to mount the candle vertically on a screen to serve as a lamp. Group Two found the problem much easier to solve. In a replication, Adamson (1952) found that only 41% of Group One solved this problem within 20 minutes, while 86% of Group Two were successful

within the time limit. It seems that, for Group One, the boxes
were framed (or defined) as "containers," while for Group Two
the boxes, since they did not contain anything, could more
easily be seen as potential platforms (a reframing for empty
boxes) upon which to stick the candle. That is, some frames
(i.e., container) are less useful in solving this platform problem than other frames (i.e., empty boxes). This leads directly
to Assumption One (see p. 23) and Assumption Five.

As suggested by Duncker's experiment, frames (ways of
seeing or defining situations) and the labels attached to them
dictate (to a greater or lesser extent) what we can see and *do*:
Our point of view determines what happens next. This seems
clear not only in art and science but also in everyday life:
Frames and their labels affect paradigm- or frame-induced
expectations and enable us to articulate and measure the
world. Any concrete "fact" can have several different labels
implying different frames (Watzlawick et al., 1974).

A Model of Complaints, Part Five

It is fully possible that the frame, "This child knows how
to have a dry bed," may be sufficient to initiate some change
in the problematic patterns. There are a variety of ways a
therapist might promote the acceptance and utilization of
this frame. The family might be asked to notice what is different on the nights before dry beds or what is different on
the mornings after dry beds, or they might be asked to each
secretly predict to themselves when the child goes to bed
whether it will be a dry night or a wet one.

The responses to these tasks, should there be any noticed
and noticeable differences, can form the basis for the next intervention, which could be assigning the differences. Or the
family might be asked to watch for signs that the dry beds
are going to continue and (since relapses do happen) any signs
that a wet bed might happen.

This gets at a rather central premise: *A minimal (although
not easy or simple) task for the therapist in the first session
at least, and perhaps in other sessions as well, is to induce*

some doubt in the clients' minds about the frames and the behaviors which follow from those frames. If the family can come to have some doubts about their perception that this child *always* wets the bed, then alternative behaviors become a real possibility. Similarly, if the family members can behave differently and *see* a difference (a dry bed), then they can also come to doubt their original framing of the situation. Frames and behaviors interact and mutually define each other: This is not an "either/or" situation.

Case Example: The Aluminum Crutch

The strength of labels was clearly described by a client who initially described her situation with these words: "I am letting my handicap cripple me." A polio victim at a young age, she wore leg braces and used a crutch to aid her walking. She believed she had adjusted to her handicap since she knew nothing else. However, she was repulsed by the type of men who were attracted to her and thought her handicap prevented her from ever having a chance for a relationship with a man she would find attractive. At the start of therapy, she described herself as being depressed about her handicap for the first time in her life. In looking at herself the way she thought others saw her and comparing herself to other attractive women her age, she found herself lacking. So, she started to make efforts whenever possible to hide her handicap by placing the crutch out of sight.

The major focus of intervention was the client's efforts to hide her crutch (de Shazer, 1979a). Once she started to *use* canes that were unusual in design, color, or shape and once she started to *display* these openly, she projected an unusual amount of strength. This new behavior made an impression on people which resulted in their treating her differently. Subsequently, she was also able to attract the kind of man she desired. As she put it during the last session, "I am no longer letting my handicap cripple me."

The label of "cripple" helped to determine her approach to people and situations, just as the new label and frame of "strength" helped to promote new and different behavior. Since the new frame elicited and promoted more rewarding responses and created expectations of more rewarding responses, she was able to maintain it.

This example points out the interactional aspects of frames and their labels. She saw other people seeing her as crippled, adopted the label, and started to behave as crippled. The more she behaved as crippled (by hiding the crutch as much as possible), the more people saw her as crippled, and the vicious cycle maintained itself. When she started to do something different (keeping her decorative canes in open view), others saw her as strong, and she started to see them see her as strong (promoting expectations of more strong behaviors), and a more virtuous cycle began to maintain itself. Importantly, a change in frames and labels can start anywhere in an interactive system. If other people had started to see her behaving in a strong way before she had seen herself doing it, then they might have initiated the "strength" frame for her. Of course, in therapy, initiating a new frame is part of the task of the therapist, and there is a need for the therapist to be reasonably sure that the new frame will fit and the new behavior will be "reinforced" by others.

A distinction needs to be drawn here. Although the effective behavior is different and appears random, the selection of what to do differently is not a matter of chance. A chance happening might be irrelevant. For instance, if her usual crutch was broken and she, therefore, used a decorative cane but continued to hide it, the difference might not be such that it made any difference in how people perceived her or in how she saw other people perceiving her. In fact, once she saw herself as strong, a return to her normal crutch in certain circumstances did not undermine the solution because she did not hide it – she was doing something differently.

Handicaps can cripple, but they can also show strength, and the difference is far from trivial. Therapy, through reframing, provides a type of mirror which can help people to see situations differently and thus behave differently. Although two (or more) labels can be applied to the same situation, all labels are not equal. Some promote detrimental behaviors while others seem to promote more beneficial behaviors.

Assumption Six

> *Brief therapists tend to give primary importance to the systemic concept of wholism: A change in one element of a system or in one of the relationships between elements will affect the other elements and relationships which together comprise the system.*

Since interactive patterns can be seen as both individual habits and "systemic" habits, it seems only reasonable that all it takes is for one person to behave differently to break the collective habit.

A Model of Complaints, Part Six

If the parents of the bed wetter are split along the lines of either (a) it is a problem or (b) it is normal, or either (a) the child is bad or (b) he is mad, or either (a) it is a physical problem or (b) it is a psychological problem, then a change in the relationship between the parents might serve to stop the bedwetting. It does not need to be the case that somehow or other the parents' fight is a "cause" of the bed-wetting or that the fights are seen as "caused" by the bed-wetting. Nor does the therapist need to see the bed-wetting as serving the function of keeping the parents together based on the premise that if they were not fighting, then they would break up. Rather, it is simply the case that the bed-wetting and the fighting are recursively related. The sequence can be punctuated as (1) the more the child wets the bed, the more the parents fight and/or (2) the more the parents fight, the more the child wets. Regardless, the sequence over time is wet bed/fight/wet bed/fight, etc. The concept of wholism suggests that stopping the fights might stop the wet beds and/or stopping the wet beds might stop the fights.

Since frames and the punctuation of sequences are related, the therapeutic approach can differ along the same lines. For instance, if the family punctuates the sequence as "wet beds lead to fights," and they frame the situation as "wet beds are the result of either madness or badness," then seeing the whole family together and interrupting the sequence by inserting some new behaviors between the time of the wet bed and the time of the fight and/or between the time of the fight and the time of the wet bed might be effective. However, seeing just the parents might not be effective since they assume the wet bed is the child's fault. In fact, seeing the child alone might be called for, particularly if the child wants to stop wetting the bed for his own reasons. If the parents use the other punctuation, which implicitly explains the wet bed as a result of parental discord, then seeing the parents without the child(ren) and stopping the fights probably would be effective, i.e., resulting in a dry bed.

In fact, the concept of wholism can be taken further. In some cases, only mother might come for therapy and describe the wet bed/fight sequence as problematic for her. She might describe her husband as not interested in getting help because he thinks the wet bed is normal and contends that if she would only agree to see things in the "right way," then both the fights and the wet beds would cease. Therefore, both are *her* complaints. In this situation the therapist might help her to change her behavior in the fight pattern and/or to change her reaction to the wet bed. Which to work on first is determined by the goals the woman and the therapist set up. If she punctuates the sequence as "wet beds lead to fights," the initial goal needs to focus on her response to the wet bed. If she punctuates the sequence as "fights lead to wet beds," then the initial goal needs to focus on her behaviors in the fight sequence. A change in her behavior vis-à-vis the wet bed might also have the ripple effect of solving the fight problem.

Creating Expectations of Change

As the BFTC team continued to work together and a distinct, unique philosophy developed, a shift occurred from our being interested in "problems/complaints and how to solve them" to "solutions and how they work." We looked at what is on the other side of the locked doors and started to figure out how we and the clients got there.

Having a team behind the mirror is almost like providing the client with more than one crystal ball to use in building a successful solution. The various team members each join with the client in constructing alternative problem realities and, therefore, alternative solutions. As a result, my colleagues and I have learned that each complaint can be constructed into many different problems that can have many possible solutions, and that any intervention which successfully prompts different behavior and/or a different way of looking at things might lead to any one of the hypothesized solutions. Sometimes the team members can agree about what to do but have different ideas about what the results might be.

Once the therapist has created (or helped to create) expectations that things are going to be different, next in importance is what the client expects to be different after the complaint is gone. That is, what you expect to happen influences what you do; therefore, if you expect something different to happen, then doing something different (to perhaps make it happen) makes sense. Of course, what you specifically want to have happen might not, but since you did something different, at least something different will happen and, therefore, you might feel more satisfied. Which door the client chooses is determined by what things he desires to be different when his complaint is resolved.

Recent work has pushed our understanding of solutions and how they work even further. In some rare cases, even when the complaint remains vaguely defined, and even when detailed goals or specific ideas about what will be different after the complaint is gone are lacking, a satisfactory solution can spontaneously develop. What seems crucial here is that solutions develop when the therapist and client are able to construct the expectation of a useful and satisfactory change. The expectation of change or the making of a different future salient to the present (Berger, Cohen, and Zelditch,

1966; de Shazer, 1978a) seems to be a skeleton key to opening the door to solution. This is not, of course, some sort of magic. It makes sense that if you know where you want to go, then getting there is easier. What does not seem so commonsensical is the idea that just *expecting* to get *somewhere different*, somewhere more satisfactory, makes it easier to get there, and just being somewhere different may be satisfactory in itself.

To sum up, the most useful way to decide which door can be opened to get to a solution is by getting a description of what the client will be doing differently and/or what sorts of things will be happening that are different when the problem is solved, and thus, creating the expectation of beneficial change. The client's language while describing some alternative futures and the details of the differences after solution seem more important than the details about the locked room of the complaint. With possible alternative futures in mind, the client can join the therapist in constructing a viable set of solutions.

CONCLUSION

The 12 building blocks of complaints and the six basic assumptions allow brief therapists to draw maps of clients' complaints in such a way that solutions to the problem can be quickly found. What the assumption and building blocks lack in detail they make up for in utility. These constructions are only high-level generalizations and seem to lack the fine detail generally suggested for problem-solving (Mayer, 1983). However, most problem-solving models seem to attempt a *match*, in von Glasersfeld's terms (1984a), between problem and solution, rather than a *fit*, and only a fit might prove necessary in experimental situations as well. On the other hand, the complaints therapists set out to solve might somehow be different from other types of problems that have been experimentally studied.

3

BINDS, LOOPS, AND
OCKHAM'S RAZOR

LEVELS OF DESCRIPTION

Conceptual maps are the foundation of our understanding about what is going on in the therapy situation. Maps tell us how to construct problems and how to get where we want to go (solutions); therefore, they are necessary for practice, research, and teaching. These maps are not the territory; they are only approximate constructions.

In general, when you watch a therapist work, what you see and hear can be described very broadly. This descriptive level is just the "top" level of what the therapist is doing. What lies behind (beneath?) the therapeutic behavior is hidden away somewhere on various levels (including assumptions, presuppositions, knowledge both implicit and explicit, world view, theory, etc.). While one level (or mode of knowing) seems more dependent on analysis, logical reasoning, calculation, and explicit description, another is more dependent on synthesis and the recognition of pattern, context, and form. Intuition and rationality are always involved to a greater or lesser extent.

Milton Erickson: A Source of Maps

Watching or reading about the work of Milton H. Erickson frequently leaves the observer wondering what has transpired, because of the apparently "intuitive" or nonrational aspects. Perhaps it is not even clear that Erickson is doing something therapeutic when he or the commentators describe how he handled a specific case. For instance, Erickson's giving the young lady with a gap between her front teeth (who was thinking seriously about suicide) the task of learning to squirt water through that gap seems absurd (in Haley, 1967b, pp. 414–417; de Shazer, 1979a). Since Erickson did not provide much information about the thinking behind his work, the reader or observer is left with a mystery. He or she does not have what Kuhn (1970) calls a "law-schema" upon which to fit the examples. That is, the observer does not have an adequate map that allows him to say, "Well, this example, Q, is just like the situation R that I am familiar with." As one continues to read Erickson's reports, it becomes clear that he did indeed have some maps or law-schema; however, their discovery (or perhaps even their invention) is left to the reader. Until the reader develops his own maps (of Erickson's maps), the reports continue to look like the tales of a shaman or wizard, since Erickson's "action-schema" did not follow the standard paradigm or standard way of thinking about human problems and solutions. Without appropriate maps (or law-schema), the reader is left with no standard of comparison.

This is similar to a complaint a man made to Picasso that his portrait of Gertrude Stein did not look like her:

> Picasso is said to have replied: "Never mind, it will." Once we have come to accept Picasso's way of seeing, have come to accept his rules of personality projection onto canvas (that linear sketches, for example, could be used to refer to things like subjects of portraits that were formerly represented by curved lines: Cubism), we too will in part see Miss Stein as Picasso drew her; interpret her, if you like, accordingly. We see the world accordingly as our existing conventions (categories, projection rules) enable us to see it. Believing is seeing (Foss, 1971, p. 235).

Similarly, the observer might complain that Erickson's therapy, as well as our own form of brief therapy, does not *look* like therapy, that is, like conventional, familiar therapy.

Starting with Haley and Weakland's efforts (Erickson, Haley, and Weakland, 1967), Erickson's work has been mapped in great detail by many map-makers, using a wide variety of map-making tools. It is tempting to think of the process as progressive and cumulative, map 2 being an improvement on map 1, and map 3 an improvement on both. However, as Kuhn has pointed out (1970), this is not always the case, particularly during a paradigm shift. The degree of fit between or among the many maps may stop at a very broad and abstract level: This map is a map of Erickson's work. For instance, a glance at Haley's and Weakland's maps (in Haley, 1967b, 1973), Bandler and Grinder's maps (1975) and de Shazer's maps (1979a) might lead the reader to wonder if the same territory is being mapped after all. Perhaps each of these is just a section map, one covering the northwest, one the southeast, and another the northeast. But this does not seem to be the case either. Haley (1973) and de Shazer (1979a) deal with some of the same case examples; even so, the maps have a relatively low level of fit.

Another way of looking at this is in terms of levels of description. On the surface level (the action-schema), there are the behaviors described by Erickson and/or the commentators. In addition to that level, there is level after level of description of that same territory (law-schema). Somehow all these maps come together, but only in the sense in which the map of the London Underground links up with the London Bus Map and these link up with the London Street Map and the water works map. Each map in its own right can help the user get where he wants to go (Wilk, 1983). They all attempt to understand and describe the processes of problem solution. It is not that one map supersedes another or that one map improves upon the other. Rather, all the maps taken together allow the user to approximate Erickson's behavior or, perhaps more correctly, his or any other's useful and successful action-schema.

Multiple Maps

Bateson (1979) suggested that this process of multiple description (of the same behavior or sequence) leads to a bonus of some sort: an idea which is of a different class than the class of descriptions (maps) used. For instance, somehow putting together Picasso's portrait of Gertrude Stein and a traditional portrait of her might prompt a bonus, an idea of what Art is, or at least an idea about the class of portraits. All the Ericksonian maps put together might prompt a bonus: an idea of what therapeutic change is all about.

Team approaches to therapy allow for some further understanding of the similarities among various maps (law-schema) and their relationship to therapist behavior (action-schema). Since the information is shared, the team's various maps fit together fairly well, and the differences between the team members' maps can be more informative than the similarities. The relationships between and among (a) map-making, (b) intervention design, and (c) therapist behavior are laid bare by the verbalization of the various law-schema, a necessary component of team cooperation. Therefore, a team approach provides the ideal field setting in which to explore the nature of clinical map-making, the foundation of this chapter. Further, this kind of study leads to additional understanding of therapeutic solutions.

COMPARATIVE MAPPING: A CASE STUDY*

This case serves to clarify the type of bonus derived from a double description: Two maps of the same territory lead to one simpler map without in the least invalidating either of the source maps. It is important to note that it is not an either/or choice or even a multiple choice; rather, it is a ques-

---

*A previous version of some of the following material appeared as part of "The Mysterious Affair of Paradoxes and Loops," written by de Shazer and Nunnally (1984).

tion of, "Which maps are or will be more useful in finding solutions?"

A couple was referred to me by a drug counselor who saw their marital problems as making the treatment for drug abuse impossible. The spouses were both using cocaine three or more times per week, which had been their pattern for over two years. The wife, "Jane," said their joint use of drugs was messing up their marriage and, therefore, she wanted to stop taking drugs to save the marriage. The marital problems were, in her view, symptoms of their drug problem. "Ralph" did not see their use of drugs as the real problem. His main concerns were their fights, some of which got physically violent, and their arguments, some about drugs. He thought that the fights and arguments needed to stop to save their marriage.

To this point, their dilemma might be described as a simple contradiction. However, their situation was not this "either/ or" even to them. Interestingly, they also shared the notions that (1) using drugs prevented boredom, which neither of them handled well, and (2) stopping drug use might lead to the breakup of their marriage, which they both valued highly, because they would have less – or maybe even *nothing* – in common.

This sort of oscillating situation (between "yes" and "no" around the drug use) has been formally described as a "double bind" (Bateson, Jackson, Haley, and Weakland, 1956; Watzlawick, Beavin, and Jackson, 1967). By plotting this couple's situation onto a double bind map, we see that this is a relationship in which

    (1) use of drugs is messing up their marriage; fights and arguments – some about drugs – are increasing;

    (2) but their use of drugs prevents boredom, so if they stop the drugs, their marriage might break up;

    (3) withdrawing from this bind might be accomplished by separating, but this is the very action they wish to avoid; also, this situation continues unresolved over time;

(4) increasing use of cocaine might provide a way to
withdraw, in a sense, by soothing them through some
of the conflicts, but then the arguments and fights,
particularly about drug use, would probably increase
and these very arguments and fights are also breaking
up the marriage.

Unless they could find some way to step outside their construction of reality, the couple seemed destined to remain in
a self-perpetuating oscillation, which could well become
lethal.

The team developed the following intervention message
which I delivered at the close of the first session:

> You've got a problem.
> It seems to us, Ralph, that your marital problems
> are being exacerbated by the drugs, or fogged over
> by the drugs, or perhaps even created by the drugs.
> Perhaps you need to, stop the drugs, just to see what
> is going on. But, on the other hand, we agree with
> you, Jane, that if you two were to, stop the drugs,
> then there might be nothing there. And, you might
> not have time to create anything before the marriage
> broke up. In short, we don't know what the fuck you
> are going to do.
> I suggest you think about what I just said, and
> decide what actions you are going to take . . . first.*

Mapped as a counter double bind (Watzlawick et al., 1967),
the intervention contains messages which convey that the
team views this as a relationship in which

(1) stopping the drugs may be necessary to save the marriage, and

---

*I wish to thank John Weakland who, while watching the videotape of this
intervention in 1981, was the first one to hear the "first" at the end of the
message, following a long pause. He pointed out that this "first" suggests
a series of actions rather than one action.

(2) not stopping the drugs may be necessary to save the marriage, and

(3) either of the above may break up the marriage,

(4) any alternative they have thought of poses great risks to the marriage, and

(5) they should take actions they have not thought of.*

By the next session, one week later, Jane and Ralph had cut their drug use by two-thirds, although their use followed the same schedule. Furthermore, without talking about it, they had initiated some new joint and separate activities. This time the main thrust of the intervention message was centered around the team's worry about a relapse.

One week later, Jane and Ralph reported that they had eliminated the drugs, that they were continuing new activities, both together and separately, and enjoying them, and that they were arguing much less. In the intervention message, we again worried about a relapse, specifically about how soon a relapse might occur.

Follow-up contact at six months and one year indicated that there had been no relapse (no drugs and only infrequent arguments). The couple also reported further improvements in their life together, as well as separately.

Although Jane and Ralph's dilemma and the interventions can be plotted *retrospectively* onto double bind maps, we have to ask ourselves: Is this particular kind of map useful in *generating* effective interventions, and could other kinds

---

*More formally within the double bind tradition, this could be mapped this way:

    (1) Within the context of therapy (which has a high survival value for their marriage),

    (2) A message is sent that (a) asserts that stopping the drugs is necessary for saving the marriage, (b) asserts that this assertion is false — stopping the drugs might break up the marriage, and (c) these are mutually exclusive.

    (3) A nonspecific series of actions is demanded (think about what you are going to do first [implying a second action at least] and do it), which is designed to promote their getting outside their either/or frame.

of maps do the job better? Over the past six or seven years
the team has found the use of double bind maps to be cumbersome and time-consuming, i.e., their construction takes longer
than the 10 to 12 minutes alloted in the hour for intervention
design. Therefore, alternative maps have been explored and
new ones developed.

A "STRANGE-LOOP" MAPPING

Cronen, Johnson, and Lannamann (1982) have developed
a new theory that considers reflexivity (oscillation) to be a
natural and necessary feature of human systems and rejects
the idea that reflexivity and paradox are coterminous. Behavior, content, episodes (interactions), relationships, life scripts,
and cultural patterns are all seen as hierarchically related and
as mutually defining one another. Some of these loops are
problematic and some are not. When the meaning of a situation cannot be determined by moving through the hierarchi-
cal levels, the situation can be described as a "strange-loop"
(Hofstadter, 1979, p. 10). A "charmed-loop," distinguished
from a strange loop, describes natural, normal, nonproblematic reflexivity. A mapping technique developed by Tomm
(1982) will be used to illustrate the application of the strange
loop description to the above case example.

If the couple's situation could be described as a charmed
loop, then the meaning of their situation could be picked from
any of the following, perhaps by moving up to another level
of the hierarchy:

(1) stopping the drugs should lead to saving the marriage,
    or
(2) not stopping the drugs should lead to break up of the
    marriage, or
(3) stopping the drugs should lead to break up of the mar-
    riage, or
(4) not stopping the drugs should lead to saving the mar-
    riage.

But the situation is not that simple: It is not charmed. Both people (and the observers) think that stopping the drugs might *either* break up the marriage *or* save the marriage, *and* both people (and the observers) think that continuing the drugs might either break up the marriage *or* save it. The couple's situation is clearly a conundrum. Each position, which seemingly should be distinct from the other, includes its opposite, which should be logically excluded: a strange loop. Within the context of this marriage, neither stopping nor continuing the drugs can "determine" staying together or breaking up. The reflexivity of the situation is such that meanings (and, therefore, actions) cannot be determined through the context in which the behaviors and episodes appear. The couple's situation can be mapped (by an observer) as in Figure 3.1.

This map is an attempt to clarify the impasse and the pragmatic effects of a strange loop. (It is important to remember that strange loops, charmed loops, and double binds do not exist. They are simply part of the map-making tools an observer brings to the observed situation: a way of organizing information. Loops are part of the map, not the territory. Like any mapping tool, loops are either useful or they are not. The description either fits the observations or it does not.) One reading of the map goes as follows: If one should want

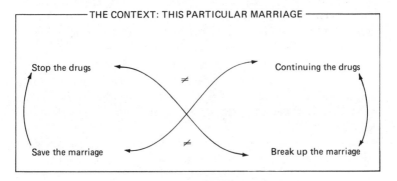

Figure 3.1   A Strange-Loop Mapping

to break up the marriage, then one should continue the drugs, but that might save the marriage, and therefore, one should stop the drugs. But stopping the drugs might save the marriage, and therefore, one should continue the drugs to break up the marriage. Another reading: If one should want to save the marriage, then one should stop the drugs, but this might break up the marriage, and therefore, one should continue the drugs.

The strange loop map is a figure 8 (on its side, which suggests the mathematical symbol for infinity) which can be read by starting at any of the four locations and then following the arrows. Clearly this map *fits* the situation the couple described and points out that the meaning of their situation cannot be determined. Therefore, the spouses are unable to make decisions or take action, since they are caught in systemic confusion. There is no way to resolve this interactional situation from inside their own construction.

This strange loop description of the couple's situation needs to be placed within the context of therapy. This context includes the therapist, the team behind the screen, and the videotaping equipment (since clients can see the camera and must give permission to tape). Furthermore, the description needs also to include the meaning given to that context, since the couple-system is now a subsystem within the therapeutic suprasystem (de Shazer, 1982a). The wife came to therapy to stop the drugs in order to save the marriage. The husband thinks that therapy is nothing but talk and that any advice will be useless. The therapist and the team, by definition, think that therapy can be useful, but they need to qualify and modify their views based on the couple's definitions and meanings. That is, for this couple, therapy needs to be more than just talk and to exclude useless advice in order to be effective.

The intervention message (repeated here for clarity) is an attempt to give new meanings to the couple's situation.

You've got a problem.

It seems to us, Ralph, that your marital problems
are being exacerbated by the drugs, or fogged over
by the drugs, or perhaps even created by the drugs.
Perhaps you need to, stop the drugs, just to see what
is going on. But, on the other hand, we agree with
you, Jane, that if you two were to, stop the drugs,
then there might be nothing there. And, you might
not have time to create anything before the marriage
broke up. In short, we don't know what the fuck you
are going to do.

I suggest that you think about what I just said,
and decide what actions you are going to take ...
first.

The team attempts to redefine the situation as one in which
some unspecified series of actions is necessary, but the action called for is neither stopping the drugs nor continuing
the drugs, because neither of these can save the marriage.
(The team does, however, imply the need to stop the drugs,
but not because that action will, or can, save the marriage.)
The team attempts to define the situation as one in which the
couple needs to "create something" in order to save the marriage and, furthermore, deliberately makes the presupposition in the last sentence that the couple is going to take action. Clearly this intervention can be seen as an attempt to
introduce new criteria about saving the marriage, a new problem construction which involves taking action or doing something different, rather than fighting about stopping or not
stopping the drugs.

In short, the intervention can be seen as based on the same
strange loop map. The reframing attempts to change the
meaning of the arrows or to disconnect the arrows so that the
recursive cycle is broken. There is some chance that the meaning is slippery enough to prompt a different response from
either husband or wife, or both. The intervention introduces
the possibility of some behavior which might make a different
enough difference.

OCKHAM'S RAZOR

William of Ockham, a 14th century philosopher, said that "what can be done with fewer means is done in vain with many," which suggests that we look for the simplest explanation that fits. This advice is extremely pertinent to therapists designing interventions. The strange loop map is no better than the counter double bind map when designing interventions, although both are useful *retrospectively*. In practice they are cumbersome and time-consuming. In the everyday world of doing therapy, there frequently is not enough time to use either map: The criteria are too complex and both are more suited to *post hoc* explanations. Both, however, are useful and valuable in map-making and theory construction.

If, as Bateson et al. (1956) maintain, the breaching of the Theory of Types is continual and inevitable in human communication, and if, as Cronen et al. (1982) maintain, this sort of reflexivity is normal and necessary, then we need Ockham's razor to simplify the clinical situation so that effective interventions can be designed within the usual clinical environment.

Mirror Images

Implicit within the double bind and counter double bind explication and within the strange loop explication is the notion that the intervention needs to be close to a *mirror image of the problem*. The criteria for a therapeutic double bind are simply the mirror image of the criteria for a pathogenic double bind; like cures like. The central premise implied by both of the above explications is that therapeutic interventions can be built on the same description (or map) as that used to describe (or map) the interaction.

The mirror concepts of pathogenic double bind and therapeutic counter double bind were first presented in "Toward a Theory of Schizophrenia" (Bateson et al., 1956). Regardless of the role the double bind plays in the etiology of problems, the double bind/counter double bind presentation is important for at least three reasons:

(1) the problem is described as happening *between* people with no reference to what might be going on *inside* them,

(2) the problem is described as happening with a *context*, which helps to define what the behaviors mean, and

(3) a treatment design (a way to prompt solution) is offered which is based on the same interactional and contextual criteria, as interpreted by the therapist (observer).

Because of the complex nature of the therapist's description, the intervention design is necessarily as complex. The double bind/counter double bind formulation is a map for mapping intervention designs which is almost the prototype for (or at least an ancestor of) the concept of *fit*.

THE CONCEPT OF FIT*

Metaphorically, the double bind/counter double bind set is like a specific key designed to fit a specific lock — there is a correspondence between elements on one map and the elements on the other map. The concept of fit, however, does not suggest this kind of correspondence. It is only that the intervention needs to fit in the way a skeleton key is designed to

---

*The essay, "An Introduction to Radical Constructivism," by Ernst von Glasersfeld (1984a) appeared while this book was taking its final form. Von Glasersfeld's notions about "fit" and the author's concept of "fit" are coincidental. Von Glasersfeld uses the following descriptive metaphor:

> A key fits if it opens the lock. The fit describes a capacity of the key, not of the lock. Thanks to professional burglars we know only too well that there are many keys that are shaped quite differently from our own but which nevertheless unlock our doors (p. 21).

The clinical concept has been described by the author (de Shazer, 1982b) and more formally with Elam Nunnally (1984) in a paper first written in 1982. The forms of the concept in this book were developed in 1983 without knowledge of von Glasersfeld's work. It is all the more interesting, therefore, that "fit" is so similarly defined (including the "key" metaphor).

be used in a variety of locks, without considering the particulars of the type or shape of lock.

A simple map based on the heuristic device (or rule of thumb) that "both/and" can be substituted for any "either/or" construction illustrates how the concept of fit can be applied to this case example (see Figure 3.2). It is the *fit* between the therapist's description of the complaint pattern and form and the map of the intervention which seems central to the process of initiating therapeutic change. That is, the couple describes the problematic behavior pattern within a certain context/meaning/frame, and then the therapeutic intervention is based on fitting within the same pattern, but with a difference due to the therapist's construction of the problem with a solution in mind.

The information from two or more different but similar maps is of a different logical type than that included in one map. The bonus or idea is only available through the information contained in the difference. For instance, there is more and different information in two descriptions of two different chess games being played than there is in either description alone. The comparison informs us of the difference between two specific games and the options of play. This helps us develop an idea of the "game of chess."

The complexities of the double bind map and of the strange loop map used to describe the above case example allow for—in fact demand—the use of Ockham's razor, because, as Wil-

Figure 3.2 Transformation Map

Complaint construction:
  EITHER drugs *OR* no drugs
  will *EITHER* save *OR* not save the marriage

Intervention construction:
  BOTH drugs *AND* no drugs
  will *BOTH* save *AND* not save the marriage

Guideline: Substituting a "BOTH/AND" construction for an "EITHER/OR" construction will promote fit and point toward a solution.

liam of Ockham would put it, such complexity is not to be used without necessity. Both descriptions involve the therapist's mapping of the same intervention pattern onto (his version of) the clients' map of the situation. Both include many of the same elements.

A bonus or idea develops: The intervention (regardless of the design principles involved) simply needs to fit within the clients' pattern (as mapped by the therapist) in such a way that the map points the way out of the oscillation. This is the simpler explanation that follows the use of multiple maps and the use of Ockham's razor. The result is the concept of *fit*, which is more general and flexible. There is no need to attempt to understand the lock in order to build an effective key when a skeleton key may work as well. To use von Glasersfeld's distinction, it is a matter of *fit* rather than *match*.

> Instead of the paradoxical requirement that knowledge should reflect, depict, or somehow correspond to a world as it might be without the knower, knowledge can now be seen as *fitting* the constraints within which the organism's living, operating, and thinking take place. From that perspective, then, "good" knowledge is the repertoire of ways of acting and/or thinking that enable the cognizing subject to organize, to predict, and even to control the flow of experience (von Glasersfeld, 1984b).

Since clients' complaints are complex constructions, it is perhaps inevitable that therapists might assume that their interventions need to be equally complex. After all, if solution were a simple matter, then clients should have found it. But, as Erickson says, clients do not know what the problem is, which, naturally, makes solution difficult. It might not be too much of an overstatement to say that a large part of this complexity is due to not having a solution in mind. What clients have tried has not been effective, so it is reasonable to assume that things will go from bad to worse, or from worse to worst, since their attempts were somehow the only "right"

way, i.e., a "bad child" needs to be punished even when the
punishment has proved ineffective.

However, the therapist does not simply receive this information as a videotape does. He interprets the client's interpretation of what is going on and constructs this interpretation on a general, goal-directed foundation: "What will a
solution look like?" That is, the therapist maps his perception
of the client's interpretation and then maps his perception of
his own interpretation. The differences between these two
maps point in the direction of the potential solutions and provide the framework for intervention design.

At first glance, it would seem reasonable, if not necessary,
for the therapist's map to be rather a lot like (the therapist's
version of) the client's map. It might seem to be just common
sense that the therapist needs to know as much as possible
about the client's complaint construction in order to effectively help the client. Based on this assumption, therapy would
necessarily be a complex, long-term endeavor. However, brief
therapy seriously challenges this assumption. Rather, it
seems that therapy can be rather limited in time and that solutions can follow very small or minimal interventions. In
fact, the intervention does not need to do more than fit
"within" the complaint construction or fit on the maps of this
construction, in order for it to have the potential of leading
to a satisfactory solution.

To return to the locked room metaphor (Chapter 2, p. 30),
each of the doors (or building blocks) has a lock, and it is the
therapist's task to find a key which leads to a solution. Rather
than trying to find the specific key for each client's particular locks, brief therapists have developed various skeleton
keys (interventions). That is, the same key has the potential
to open various doors and the same door can be opened with
various keys. This means that we do not need to know very
much about specific locks, at least in any detail. Perhaps all
we need to know is the way locks work.

A more formal way of describing the principles of intervention design can be based on this concept of fit. The intervention design needs to be constructed upon:

(1) the therapist's interpretation or perception of the pattern of the complaint *and/or*

(2) the therapist's perception of the client's framing of the complaint in such a way that solution can readily develop. The design needs to *fit* in such a way that

(3) it is capable of fitting on the same map used to map the problem *and/or*

(4) it is capable of fitting within (the map of) the client's world view, but with a difference that – at least potentially – makes a difference, i.e., leads to a satisfactory solution.

The complaints clients make to therapists are intricate constructions involving behaviors (bits and sequences), the context of those behaviors, the meanings they attach to those behaviors in that context, their goals (both specific and general), their more general world view, and other components, including their attempts and the attempts of others to solve the problem. Given the potential for complexity in the clinical situation, it is remarkable that sometimes both clients and therapists can agree that their efforts have been successful. Failure might be the more reasonable expectation. The concept of fit is designed to both utilize this complexity and to minimize the potential confusion due to overly intricate constructions.

Watzlawick (1984) provides a useful metaphor.

A captain who on a dark, stormy night has to sail through an uncharted channel, devoid of beacons and other navigational aids, will either wreck his ship on the cliffs or regain the safe, open sea beyond the strait. If he loses ship and life, his failure proves that the course he steered was not the right one. One may say that he discovered what the passage was *not*. If, on the other hand, he clears the strait, this success merely proves that he literally did not at any point come into collision with the (otherwise unknown) shape and nature of the waterway; it tells him nothing about how safe or how close to disaster he was at any moment. He passed the strait like a blind man. His course *fit* the unknown topography, but this does not mean that it *matched* it – if we take matching in von Glasersfeld's sense, that is, that the course matched the real configuration of the channel. It would not be too difficult to imagine that the *actual* shape of the strait might offer a number of safer and shorter passages (p. 15).

In much the same way, it is only necessary that a therapeutic intervention *fit* the constructed problem in such a way that the goal is reached, i.e., a solution develops. This tells us nothing about how other interventions might have fit the client's problem construction in other ways and reached the same goal. Likewise, it tells us nothing about other therapeutic problem constructions which might have been built with the same components and how some other intervention might have fit that problem in such a way that it would have led to the same solution or a different but equally successful solution. The concept of fit is designed to give the therapist satisfactory options for promoting therapist-client cooperation based on the idea that useful problem constructions vary according to which components go into the therapeutic problem construction (i.e., behaviors, contexts, frames, etc.) and the built-in goal of the endeavor. In order for the therapeutic problem construction to be useful, it must include at least a potential solution.

4

A COOPERATING MODE
OF THERAPY

In Chapter 3, two theories concerned with clinical issues –
the double bind and the strange loop – were used binocularly
to explicate the same case material, resulting in the concept
of "fit." In this chapter, two well researched theories – Axelrod's theory of cooperation (1984) and Berger's expectation
states theory (Berger et al., 1977) – will be used similarly to
look at the therapeutic context and the therapist's stance.

CONSTRUCTING A THERAPEUTIC REALITY

Change can be defined in a clinical context as:

> A therapeutic process of initiating (and promoting)
> observed *new* and *different* behaviors and/or percep-
> tions (frames) within the context of the presenting
> problem (and the patterns which surround it) and/or
> the solution of that problem (de Shazer and Molnar,
> 1984a) (keeping in mind that the patterns which sur-
> round the problem and the problem itself are not two
> separate "things" but are recursively related aspects
> of the same "thing").

That is, therapeutic change is an interactional process involving both client and therapist. It is not something the
therapist does to clients as though clients were some sort of

passive recipients. Therapy is not akin to surgery or TV repair—except that once a TV is fixed, one can expect it to again need fixing at a later date, which does not mean that the first repair job was insufficient. Moreover, clients do not bring their problems in a box neatly labeled "problem of type x." Rather, when clients present their problem to the therapist, they are already in the process of redefining those problems (Emerson and Messinger, 1977).

Clients and therapist can be seen as together constructing a problem reality. From this perspective, clients can be seen as initiating the change process by the very act of bringing their problem to a therapist, thus making it public. This makes the definition of the problem subject to change. Since the clients have at least implicitly stated that the problem is one they cannot solve, the new definition needs to be such that a solution is possible. Clients are stuck with certain world views; one sees the half glass of water as half-full, while another sees it as half-empty. Obviously, the therapist will not find a solution by agreeing with one that the glass is half-full or with the other that it is half-empty. If that were a solution, the clients would have found it. Likewise, declaring that both are equally wrong might only make both parties more rigid in their views. It seems more useful to construct a more solvable problem; for example, the therapist might declare that both are right, which will promote a fit, and then wonder how two rights can cause such trouble.

According to Milton Erickson,

> . . . patients that come to you, come to you because they don't *know* exactly WHY they come. They have problems, and if they knew what they WERE they wouldn't *have come*. And since they don't know what their problems REALLY are they can't tell you. They can only tell you a rather confused account of what they think. And you listen with YOUR background and you don't know what they are saying, but you better know that you don't know. And then you need to do SOMETHING that induces a *change* in the

patient . . . any little change, because that patient
wants a change, however small, and he will accept
that AS a change. He won't stop to measure the EX-
TENT of that change. He will accept that as a change
and then he will follow that change and the change
will develop in accord with his own *needs* . . . It's
much like rolling a snowball down a mountainside. It
starts out a small snowball, but as it rolls down it
gets larger and larger . . . and it becomes an avalanche
that fits the shape of the mountain (in Gordon and
Meyers-Anderson, 1981, pp. 16–17).

It seems reasonable, therefore, that therapists think about the
interactional activity of therapy as a cooperative endeavor in
which therapist and clients jointly construct a problem that
can be solved.

COOPERATING

A decision tree (de Shazer, 1982a) has been developed to
map the sequences of interaction between the clients' reported
response to a task and therapists' assignment of a task; this
tree suggests to therapists how to respond to the clients' responses in the best way to promote cooperating and thus solutions (see Figure 4.1).

Simply, if in the first session the therapist gave a concrete
homework assignment and that task was performed by the
client in a straightforward manner (that is, the intervention
achieved a fit), then it is most useful, in that situation, for the
therapist to again give a concrete homework assignment: The
therapist cooperates by doing what the client did with the
previous task. However, if the client reports not performing
the task, then it is more useful to cooperate and promote fit
by not giving that client another concrete task in that session.
Or, if the client's response is a modification of the assigned
task, then it seems better that the therapist give an easily
modifiable task or one that includes options or choices, because the client will probably find that it fits. If the client's

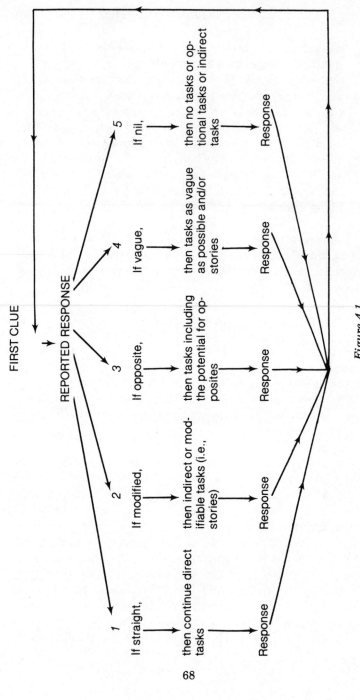

Figure 4.1

68

report is vague or confused, then the therapist's task, in response, needs to be similarly vague or confused. In addition to fitting (i.e., the therapist's response can be mapped within the scope of the map of the client's response), each of these therapist responses needs to be different enough to make a difference. In principle, this is similar to TIT FOR TAT (see below) in that the therapist promotes or achieves fit by responding in kind to the client's response.

When punctuated in this way, the first session can be seen as "diagnostic." The therapist tries to figure out the client's manner of cooperating and then gives an intervention based on the "diagnosis." The client's report in the following session informs the therapist about the client's manner of cooperating and the degree of fit. Then, if necessary, the therapist modifies the approach in response.

A Shift in Punctuation

Over the years, we have shifted the punctuation and emphasis at the Brief Family Therapy Center. Instead of the therapists' simply assuming that a particular cooperating response by a client calls for a particular type of cooperating response by the therapist, or instead of viewing cooperating as if initiated and defined by the client's responses (de Shazer, 1982a), BFTC therapists now assume that initiating and promoting responsive behavior is their task. Therefore, the emphasis in the first session is on establishing rapport and developing or promoting cooperating. That is, the therapist can be seen to make the first cooperating move(s). Of course, the client's response in the subsequent session informs the therapist about the fit that is developing. This emphasis is more consistent with our view that change is an inevitable and continual process. Given this emphasis, what the therapist needs to do is shape the change process in such a way that clients can solve the problems they bring to therapy.

As long as the therapist cannot not influence the process of change because the observer influences the observed, it seems that that influence in the therapeutic context needs to be constructively used to create for the client the expectation of noticeable change – which is what the therapist is paid to do.

A Theory of Cooperation

Robert Axelrod (1984; Axelrod and Hamilton, 1981) has done some work that is pertinent in this context. He held two computer tournaments during which the Prisoner's Dilemma game was played.

One player gets to pick a row (cooperate or defect), while simultaneously the other player gets to pick a column (cooperate or defect). There are four possible results: (1) if both cooperate, each gets 3 points; (2) if the row player cooperates, but the column player defects, then the row player gets 0 points and the column player gets 5; (3) if the row player defects and the column player cooperates, then the row player gets 5 while the column player gets 0; and (4) if both defect, then each gets 1 point (see Figure 4.2).

When this game is played once or any known finite number of times, the best strategy seems to be defection, since the player has a chance of getting the maximum payoff of 5 points (Axelrod, 1984, p. 10). When, however, the players are going to continue to play each other indefinitely, another strategy pays off best for both: cooperating. Axelrod (p. 3) used computer tournaments to study the problem of coopera-

Figure 4.2 The Prisoner's Dilemma Game

| | | Column player | |
		cooperate	defect
Row player	cooperate	$r = 3, r = 3$	$s = 0, t = 5$
	defect	$t = 5, s = 0$	$p = 1, p = 1$

tion, asking, "Under what conditions will cooperation emerge in a world of egoists without central authority?"

The game "is an elegant embodiment of the problem of achieving mutual cooperation, and therefore provides the basis for" their analysis (Axelrod and Hamilton, 1981, p. 1391). During the first tournament a program called TIT FOR TAT (developed by Anatole Rapoport) proved the winner. TIT FOR TAT was the shortest program (four lines): "This strategy is simply one of cooperating on the first move and then doing whatever the other player did on the preceding move" (Axelrod and Hamilton, 1981, p. 1391). If the other player defected, then on the following move so did TIT FOR TAT; the same when the other player cooperated. Hofstadter (1983), describing this work, thinks that

> the summarized lesson of the first tournament seems to have been that it is important to be *nice* ("Do not be the first to defect"), and *forgiving* ("Do not hold a grudge once you have vented your anger"). TIT FOR TAT has both qualities (p. 22).

More players were invited for a second round; all were aware of the results of the first tournament and all knew TIT FOR TAT's strategy. However, most of the participants in the second tournament had not really learned the importance of being willing to initiate and reciprocate cooperation. TIT FOR TAT won again. Even very tricky and complicated programs designed to take advantage of TIT FOR TAT were defeated in the long run. TIT FOR TAT won by eliciting cooperation or mutually rewarding outcomes rather than by beating the other players. Both TIT FOR TAT and the other programs did well.

From this second tournament another key concept emerged: *provocability*—the idea that one should retaliate when the other had defected. This sort of success by such a simple program needs explaining. In addition to being nice, provocable, and forgiving, TIT FOR TAT is also very simple and straightforward. Too much complication can seem obscure, chaotic, random, or simply confused. Thus even computer programs, which are without feelings about other programs, behave in such a way that cooperative behavior – behavior that is mutually beneficial – is elicited. Both programs, TIT FOR TAT and its opponent, do well in the game. As Axelrod points out, TIT FOR TAT does not play "against opponents" but, rather, with other players. This distinction is not trivial (de Shazer, 1982b). When playing against opponents the idea is that one "wins" and the other "loses," but when playing with another player the idea is to work toward success for both. TIT FOR TAT's response pattern fits with the other players' patterns.

Interactions between computer programs are not identical to those among humans and within human systems, such as the therapeutic system. Nonetheless, when the patterns can be, to some extent, usefully compared, then we can learn something.

Therapist-Client Cooperation

The family resemblance between the decision tree and TIT FOR TAT is rather striking when this response-to-response therapeutic approach is placed within its context, the concept of cooperating:

> Each family (individual or couple) shows a unique way of attempting to cooperate, and the therapist's job becomes, first, to describe that particular manner to himself that the family shows and, then, to cooperate with the family's way and, thus, to promote change (de Shazer, 1982a, pp. 9–10).

Instead of assuming resistance (de Shazer, 1979c, 1982a, 1984), i.e., client against therapist or change vs. no change, this approach assumes cooperating: The therapist responds to the client's response to the task with a response of the same type (i.e., TIT FOR TAT). It should be kept in mind that "resistance" is only a metaphor for describing certain behaviors in the therapy context and that other metaphors can be more useful. "Resistance" is not something concrete.

The relationship between the concept of "resistance" and the concept of "cooperating" might be seen in this way: If a therapist *chooses* to see the clients' behavior as resistance, then their attempts to cooperate cannot be seen, since each view precludes the other; if a therapist is looking for cooperative behavior, then he will be unable to see resistance. That is, both concepts or levels of description can address different aspects of the same behaviors. Mixing the two descriptions results in the sort of confused tangle that typically comes from mixing descriptions based on different classes.

As with TIT FOR TAT in the tournaments, therapist behavior of a cooperating sort is seen as eliciting, promoting, and/or prompting cooperating behavior by the client as therapist and client jointly construct a problem that can be solved. Axelrod (1984, p. 126) suggests that "mutual cooperation can be stable if the future is sufficiently important relative to the present," which is certainly true of the therapy situation. Of course, for the therapist, the choice is not just simply *either* defect *or* cooperate. Rather, the client's response defines, more or less, what "cooperation" is going to mean, or it describes the degree of fit in the context of the particular relationship; it is TIT FOR TAT, do what they did, rather than the either/or choice. This allows the therapist to achieve some sort of fit between his intervention and the complaint. The interactional nature of the concept of cooperating recognizes the "impossibility of separating the scientific observer from the observed phenomena" (Capra, 1977, p. 266). Cooperating is a descriptive metaphor applied to the *relationship*, rather than to either of the subsystems involved.

TIT FOR TAT *presupposed* cooperation from the start. On the first move it cooperated before knowing what the other player might do, and it was never the first to defect. TIT FOR TAT could not know what the other program might do. However, TIT FOR TAT did "manipulate" things in such a way that cooperation was possible. This strategy might be seen as a move prompted by TIT FOR TAT's blind faith in the potential goodness of the other programs. Some might see TIT FOR TAT as being rather naive and optimistic. (After all, the other player might play dirty and defect or might resist TIT FOR TAT's goodwilled gesture.) However, mean, nasty, tricky programs and even random programs all lost to TIT FOR TAT during the long interaction of the tournament. Cooperation proved an effective strategy for winning the games without defeating the opponent.

The shift in emphasis at BFTC also presupposes cooperating. Rather than waiting to define cooperating by what the client reports as his response to the previous session's task, the therapist attempts to establish conditions under which cooperating will be promoted in the very first session.

EXPECTATIONS OF CHANGE

Expectation states theory* (Berger et al., 1974) is concerned with both how interactional situations develop and maintain patterns and also how the expectation-maintaining behaviors change. The theory is seen as applying in situations which meet two scope conditions: The people who are interacting (1) have a task orientation and (2) are collectively oriented. Therapy based upon a cooperative relationship between therapist and client that has the present and the future as a focus demands that this joint endeavor have a shared goal. In this framework, therapy sessions become both task oriented and collectively oriented; thus, they can be seen as fitting within the scope of the theory. Therapist and client are engaged in a task that they can complete successfully or unsuccessfully, and only a relatively specific goal can be used for measurement of this. Together, they are working to solve some problem. Therefore, having a goal or goals means that there is some expected useful outcome(s) for their efforts. Since therapeutic endeavor is collective, each individual needs

---

*The use of expectation states theory in this book is not, in any formal sense, an application, nor is the therapy material offered as further proof of the theory. Simply, the theory is used to explicate one way of constructing the therapeutic reality. The theory offers a point of view based on rigorous, experimental studies. The interpretation offered here is mine based on collaborative work with Joseph Berger.

to take into account the others' opinions in solving the problem or completing the task.

It would seem reasonable that when clients bring their complaints to therapy their expectations for the future include the idea that things can only go from bad to worse, since they have repeatedly attempted solutions which have failed. Each failed attempt builds up expectations for continued failure. Clients develop a self-evaluation as a person having an insolvable complaint, and this evaluation carries over from one situation to the next similar one. As these similar situations continue over time, the clients receive information (or evaluations for themselves and others) that can be interpreted as a sure sign that the insolvable complaint is continuing. That is, each repeat of the complaint situation helps to build expectations that the next time a similar situation is approached the results will be something to complain about: the same damn thing over and over again.

Change in the structure of these expectations will occur when the conditions change in some way, but the process itself generates expectation-maintaining behaviors. Feedback or evaluation from an authoritative source such as a therapist can undermine these expectations and thus promote changes in behavior, different outcomes, and the development of new expectations (Berger et al., 1977). Of course, these new expectations will also be self-maintaining and the clients stand a chance of a more satisfactory life.

A Model

For instance, we have all met couples who are constantly arguing. Each time, they promise themselves, each other, parents, in-laws, friends, and neighbors that this will be the last argument. But, time after time, they return to arguing. From this perspective, it is not necessary that there be something about the arguing that serves as a reward or reinforcement and thereby undermines the efforts to quit. All that is needed to undermine the success of the venture is that previous failures to quit have built up in each of them, as well as in others in their lives, the expectation that they will again fail to quit.

When the therapist helps the arguing couple to describe life together after these arguments are no longer something to complain about, complete with the therapist's open expectation that this future is a good possibility, then the first steps toward a new set of expectations have been taken. Each change the couple makes, i.e., anything the couple does that is good for them whether it is part of the complaint or not, is evaluated positively (in the compliments phase of the intervention message) by the therapist (who, as expert, becomes a temporary, significant other in their system) as another step toward this more satisfactory future. This positive evaluation of any changes helps to build the expectation that this future, which is salient to the couple as a couple, is beginning. Once these expectations are created, a more satisfactory life is possible and problematic arguments are less likely. Of course, any couple is going to disagree and argue now and then. The therapeutic change in this situation might be that any subsequent arguments will no longer be problematic, i.e., they can be seen by the couple as just a normal part of life. Under these conditions, the couple stands a good chance of arguing far less often.

In this case, the solution is built around the way the spouses describe life after the arguments are no longer problematic. Of course, there are many different ways each could change individually and/or they could change collectively so that this future would become a reality. Thus, the solution is really unpredictable. Therefore, the specific and concrete goal for this couple might just be a certain period of time without a typical, troublesome argument, which would indicate to them that they stand a good chance of success at this endeavor of making life together more satisfactory. Or, a goal might be constructed around their getting through a particularly troublesome type of event without an argument. In any case, there are various routes, using various techniques, that the therapist can help the couple take to a solution of a more satisfactory future.

The Process of Building Expectations

Since solutions are not predictable in any detail and since there is more than one potential way of behaving in the future without the complaint, the new set of expectations can be constructed out of any satisfactory or beneficial changes. Any change stands a chance of starting a ripple effect which will lead to a more satisfactory future. Therefore, the brief therapist reacts to any change as an indication that things are starting to go right for the clients. It does not seem to matter if a particular change is new or different behavior, or if it is an exception to the rules of the complaint, or even if it seemingly has nothing to do with the complaint. Any change is a difference that could well prove to be different enough to be part of the solution. In any case, any change can become part of the construction of a new set of expectations that will be part of creating the solution.

Any spontaneous change, one that is generated by the clients and is not part of a specific, therapeutic directive such as, "next time x happens, do y," suggests that some sort of fit has been achieved. Further, any spontaneous change can be constructed as part of the solution by the therapist. Of course, since any change helps to promote expectations of further change, fit will be easier to achieve in future interventions.

Although a specific behavioral change may be the stated goal, the expectation that is being constructed involves not only that one bit of behavior but also other members of the same class of behaviors. Any member of that class of behaviors may start a similar kind of ripple effect. Since a specific change is almost impossible to predict, what the therapist is after is a change in the context or context markers which will promote what the client expects to be different as a result of reaching or achieving the specific goal. Of course, achieving the specific goal of resolving the clients' complaint is frequently a part of the change in context or the change in the class of which the complaint behavior is a member. The couple may continue to have arguments but, because of a change in the context or meaning of those arguments (which are now in some nonproblematic class), they will not find it necessary to complain.

A PRESENT AND FUTURE STANCE

As can be readily seen, these theories help to explicate the therapeutic context. According to Erickson,

> the purpose of psychotherapy should be to help the patient in the most adequate, available and acceptable fashion. In rendering him aid, there should be full respect for and utilization of whatever the patient presents. Emphasis should be placed more on what the patient does in the present and will do in the future than on a mere understanding of why some long-past event occurred. *The sine qua non of psychotherapy should be the present and the future* adjustment of the patient (in Haley, 1967b, p. 406, emphasis added).

Haley described Erickson's application of this line of thought in this way:

> Erickson appears to approach each patient with an expectation that change is not only possible but *inevitable.* There is a sureness which exudes from him, although he can be unsure if he wishes, and an attitude of confidence as if it would *surprise* him *if change did not occur* (Haley, 1967a, p. 535, emphasis added).

The assumptions behind Erickson's focus on the present and future of his patients and on the inevitability of change were probably different from the assumptions behind the theory of cooperation and expectation states theory. Nevertheless, Erickson's therapeutic stance can readily be explicated with these two theories.

Additionally, this view seems related to a Buddhistic notion about change. For the Buddhist (Stcherbatsky, 1962) change is a continual process and stability is only an illusion or a memory of one moment during the process of change.

Clearly, there are differences (changes) which make a difference, as well as changes which do *not* make a difference. In the latter case, some changes are not perceived as differences because they are too small or so slow that they contain no news of difference – the Buddhistic illusion of stability.

The therapist's behavior depends on his stance or on how he frames and defines the clinical situation. At BFTC it is part of the therapist's task to help define the context of therapy and create certain expectations of problem solution. Such expectations, once formed, help to determine what one sees as happening and, therefore, what *is* happening (Berger et al., 1977). At BFTC, clinical practice defines therapy as cooperative, as oriented toward change and solutions, and as focused on the present and future.

Axelrod's and Berger's studies suggest that cooperation and change can be promoted through linking the future to the present. Both might well be seen as experimental verifications of the principles behind the crystal ball technique (Erickson, 1954b; de Shazer, 1978a). When the future is salient to the present and a positively held goal is established, current behaviors and current events in life can be reconstructed as part of the process of reaching the goal. The past, particularly the problematic areas of the past, can then be seen as potentially detrimental to solution. Of course, past successes, deliberate or accidental, can be used in constructing a solution.

The stance used at BFTC attempts to define the clients' situation as one in which the therapist (and/or team) expects change to happen – and to happen quickly. Of course, this assumption is frequently the opposite of the clients' expectation. Within this frame, any intervention even implicitly focused on change in the immediate future lets the client know that the therapist expects change and is sure that change will occur. The therapist, like TIT FOR TAT, makes a cooperating move before the client has shown any response to a task.

As Erickson put it in 1965:

to elicit the cooperation of the patient one ought to be permissive for best results. One really ought to ask the patient to cooperate in achieving a common goal. You should keep in mind that that common goal is a goal for the welfare of the patient wherein the patient is cooperating with you to achieve something that primarily is of benefit to him. He cooperates with the surgeon primarily to get over whatever the condition is (Erickson and Rossi, 1983, p. 166).

5

THE CRYSTAL BALL
TECHNIQUE

MAKING THE FUTURE SALIENT TO THE PRESENT

Erickson developed the crystal ball technique and described using it occasionally with a variety of problems (1954b). Since mid 1974, I have used my version with clients who have had sexual complaints but no active partner or a partner who was unwilling to participate in the therapy. During the past several years I have also used the procedure with other kinds of complaints. The crystal ball technique is used to project the client into a future that is successful: The complaint is gone. I have found that simply having the client, while in a trance, view his or her future in a crystal ball or a series of crystal balls can be enough to prompt different behavior, thereby leading to a solution (de Shazer, 1978a). The ideas behind the technique can also be used in clinical situations that do not involve a formal trance. Either way, the client constructs his own solution, which can then be used to guide the therapy. As I see it, the principles behind this technique form the foundation for therapy based on solutions rather than problems.

THE TECHNIQUE

As I originally developed it, the procedure involves the client's viewing several different crystal balls. In the first one, I ask him or her to visualize and fully experience an early, pleasant memory that was forgotten long ago. While still in a trance, the client is asked to describe this memory in as much detail as possible, paying particular attention to what other people are doing. Then this memory is returned "to where it had been all these years" and the client is brought out of the trance.

This first step is designed to teach the client (a) to develop crystal balls, (b) to pay attention to his or her own behavior and the behavior of others, and (c) to encourage the idea that forgotten things can be remembered while remembered things can be forgotten. As many crystal balls as necessary can be used to train the client to observe his or her own behavior and the responsive behavior of others. People evaluate themselves and their performance in large part based on how they see others seeing them (Mead, 1934; Shibutani, 1961; Webster and Sobieszek, 1974). An important part of the crystal ball technique is built on predicting the reactions a difference will make to the other people involved in the client's life. The predicted reactions help the client to change his or her own expectations and thus change the behaviors. Once I am satisfied with the client's learning, the trance is interrupted. In order to encourage amnesia for the experience, I then lead the conversation back to any topic we had discussed before the trance. When the procedure was originally developed, I would let this conversation continue for a time before asking any questions about the trance experience. My idea was to "test" for amnesia, which I then thought was an important element to the successful use of the procedure. Currently, however, I think that amnesia is unimportant to the success of the technique.

Originally, the second step involved reestablishing the trance so that the client could use a different crystal ball to remember a recent but *surprisingly* forgotten event, some event the client wished to remember more clearly. Currently, the second crystal ball is used for the client's remembering *some success* in life, particularly one that is an exception to the rules surrounding the complaint. In either case, I ask the client to describe his or her own behavior and the behavior of the other people involved in the situation. I then return to the topic of conversation used after the first trance as a way to reorient the client before the session is ended.

In the first and second steps the crystal balls are used to look into the past and to experience remembering, forgetting, and observing the reactions of other people, as well as to awaken the feeling of success. These first two steps are also training for the third and fourth steps, when the crystal balls are used to look into the future.

The third step seems to be the most important one. During this, the client is oriented to the future. At first the passage of time is described in some detail and then it becomes progressively more vague. By the time the client is asked to look into the crystal ball, I am giving no clues about any specific date or hour. I then ask the client to *remember* returning to tell me about the successful resolution of the problem.

In the fourth step, I ask the client to use another crystal ball for *remembering* the manner in which the problem was solved, his or her reactions to this process, and the reactions of the other people involved. I then reorient the client to the present and pick up some topic of conversation that has nothing to do with the crystal balls or the presenting problem. When the session is over, I have to sit back and sometimes wait for months to find out what happened. Most often the client reports a *different* process of solving the problem than the one imagined in the fourth crystal ball.

People vary in their ability to use trance and for some the training necessary for this procedure can take several sessions. Although some of my clients come expecting hypnosis and trance to be used, others have different expectations. For some, trance and hypnosis are magic. I have, consequently, developed a crystal ball technique that can be used without trance inductions and without the mention of hypnosis.

As the usefulness of the third and fourth steps became clear to us, my colleagues and I started to ask all our clients, "What will things be like for you and others when the problem is solved?" This question has become a standard theme of our initial interview. Many clients are able to peer into crystal balls *without* using a trance and are able to construct similar expectations for a future without the complaint. What seems to matter is that once the client has a picture of success (life after the complaint is gone), he can spontaneously do something different so that this vision of the future (or some other, equally satisfying future) can be come reality. Since successful prediction is so difficult in human affairs, it is frequently better for therapist and client to construct alternative ways in which the client will know when the problem is solved.

Case Example: Afraid of What?

Mrs. Hart wanted hypnosis because hypnosis had helped her mother quit smoking after 35 years. A young mother of three children under age six, she came to therapy because her mother would no longer take her to the grocery store in order to protect her from panic attacks. Mrs. Hart, ever since the divorce three years earlier, had had her mother, her neighbors, or her friends take her shopping. Now she was afraid she would ruin her friendships and the neighbors would shy away from her because her fear of panic attacks was growing. It was no longer just grocery stores she feared, but any place with a lot of people.

Her fears were interfering more and more with her life and she was starting to feel lonely. But she could not go out to meet men because she feared the situations in which meeting men was possible. In fact, since the two panic attacks quite soon after the divorce, she had not put herself in any situations where an attack was possible: She always had someone take her or do it for her.

Steps one and two took most of three sessions. At first her crystal balls were like movies someone else had taken of her. Even after she learned to see other people in the crystal balls, she found it difficult to describe what was going on while in a trance or out of trance. Once I was satisfied that she was experiencing these successful situations as social and interactive, I did not ask for any further descriptions.

In the fifth session, I went on to steps three and four. She had some difficulty with the fourth step and spontaneously came out of the trance but reentered on her own. At the end of the session she smiled and thanked me, adding, "You know when the next session will be." The following week she called and reported a trip to the grocery store during which she felt that a panic was continually trying to develop but she did not let it. Six weeks later she came to tell me about her continued success. By the third trip to the grocery store, she was no longer aware of any fears. She found it rather amusing that it was not the grocery store she saw in the crystal ball and that the solution was far easier than she had imagined.

Case Example: Batter Up!

Mr. Reilly, a young professional, came to therapy because he had been unable to achieve an erection for almost five years. Two years earlier, he and his wife divorced when she moved to the West Coast to pursue her career. In part, he blamed the divorce on his erectile difficulty and he blamed the sexual dysfunction on her career development while they were still married. He had expected that after the divorce, when he started to become more active socially, he would have no erectile problems. This did not turn out to be the case. During most of this five-year period he had been in therapy either with his ex-wife or by himself. Although he no longer felt depressed, he still had this problem, which led him to seek hypnosis.

Prior to this five-year period, Mr. Reilly never had any difficulty achieving or maintaining erections. In fact, sex had been good between him and his ex-wife until the third year of their marriage. He thought about his problem more and more, he discussed it frequently with his therapist, and he discussed it with the two women whom he had dated for some time. They all had come to the conclusion that he resented his ex-wife's career and maybe even hated women. He did not like this conclusion and was determined to solve his problem to prove them wrong.

Mr. Reilly tried so hard to achieve a trance that he got in his own way and it was not until the third session that we found a useful approach. He was a member of a softball team that took play seriously. Their leading hitter in previous seasons, he had been dropped from third to eighth in the batting order because of his season-long slump. They had even taken videotapes of his struggles, which he was watching in order to figure out what he was doing wrong. I told him that it seemed to me that they were going about it in the wrong way: What he needed to do was watch himself getting hits. But they had no tapes of success.

The induction was initiated by having him close his eyes and imagine being in the batter's box. I then suggested he experience more and more of the sights, sounds, and smells associated with this. As this continued, I suggested he experience all of the physical sensations of being in the batter's box. The session ended after he was able to reexperience having hit a double.

Over the weekend his hitting returned to normal, and when he came for the next session he was ready to go into a trance. Again, the induction dealt with his remembering getting a hit and feeling successful. A new crystal ball was used so that he could remember successful sex. At the end of the session he remarked, "If this crystal ball works like the other one, the problem will be solved tonight!" I suggested that we better set some odds on it because it "was certainly not a sure thing."

Unfortunately, his date had to cancel and he did not have an opportunity before the next session to put this to the test. At that session we used the crystal ball to predict success at some undetermined point in the future. Another crystal ball was used to review the successes and failures that he had had on the way to knowing the problem is solved. Since Mr. Reilly tried so hard, I was afraid he would interpret any failure along the way as a sign of defeat, so it was particularly important to mention failures as part of the route to success.

It was a month before he called to report his first success, which had followed two more failures. One year later he and his future wife came to see about some difficulties they were having with their children. At that point they reported continued sexual success.

Case Example: Jake's Girl*

Jake sent Polly to therapy so that she could work on her jealousy. After finding out that she too considered the jealousy to be a problem, I asked her, "How will Jake know that the problem is solved?" It turned out Jake was a very quiet person, capable of being with a group for hours without saying a word. This was OK with Polly, but she did not like it when any of his few words were given to another woman. Then she would blow up, cause a scene, and go home. Therefore, Jake would know the problem was solved when he could talk to another woman in front of Polly without her blowing up. I wondered if she needed to change her feelings or if it would be OK with Jake if she just showed her jealousy less. She thought that he would not know the difference and so just showing it less would be enough.

At this point Polly was in town just for the purpose of getting therapy and her only contact with Jake was by telephone. They thought therapy would save their relationship and they planned on her returning home once she had cured her jealousy. Since they were not going to see each other, I was puzzled about how either of them would know it was time for her to go home. Polly thought that the best sign would be if she made an unscheduled call home and did not get upset if Jake was not there to answer. Interestingly, Jake had never given her any cause for being jealous except talking to other women in front of Polly. Inquiring about the rest of the pattern, I found out that Jake did not give Polly the attention she wanted. She was sure that deep inside he loved her but for some reason he was unable to show it. After the break, I relayed the following message from the team, which is based on the first steps of the crystal ball technique:

---

*Adele and Lyman Wynne were guest members of the team for the first session of this case.

First of all, we're impressed that you and Jake care
enough about each other to agree to take this time
to work on changing how you show what you've called
jealousy. We think this "jealousy" is really one of the
ways you show your love and affection for Jake. In
fact, we think that you are showing all the affection
for both of you.

As we thought about what you said, we started to
wonder: If you stopped showing so much affection in
public, how would other people know you two belong
to each other?

Between now and next time, we want you to *remember* and *think* about the various ways Jake has
of showing the affection he has inside *and* when and
where he is comfortable enough showing that to you.

Three days later, after a weekend, she came to the second
session and described in great detail the rare occurrences
when Jake showed affection to her. She remembered these
with fondness and was glad we had given her that task because she had forgotten several events. Furthermore, she
thought that his confidence in her as a business partner was
a further sign that he cared. They found working together so
rewarding that she would be willing to give up the love relationship if it was necessary to maintain the business relationship. As she thought about this over the weekend, she had
decided that we were right: The real problem was that Jake
did not show affection and she had been trying to use the
jealousy to provoke his showing it. She would know this problem was solved when Jake spontaneously showed some affection or said, 'I love you." We then explored some of the
tools she might use to help bring out the affection she knew
was inside him. After the break I relayed the following message, which again called for the use of crystal balls:

First of all, we wonder what would happen when
you do not show any "jealousy" in order to protect
your business relationship. Jake might respond. How-

ever, we think that just being passive is not enough because, we are afraid, Jake will think it is a sign that you've lost interest.

Second, perhaps you need to act mysterious enough to provoke *his* jealousy without your actually doing anything.

Third, perhaps you need to be passive *and* seductive which could draw out his affections.

Between now and next session, we want you to think about what differences each of these three changes will make to how you and Jake get along. Figure out how he will react when you are doing something different.

Three days later she returned. After looking at the three crystal balls the evening after the second session and developing ideas about how Jake would react, she found another crystal ball – a future which did not include Jake. At first this idea was shocking, but the more she thought about it, the more relief she felt: If he did not love her, she did not have to stay with him. After more careful thought, she decided she was not going to say "I love you" during their next phone call and see if he noticed the difference. Furthermore, she decided that after this session she was going to go home. If he did not spontaneously show affection, then she would know that she had been wrong about his feelings toward her. She certainly was not going to show affection for him and was not going to be seductive or mysterious. If he did not feel the need to show her affection, she was no longer going to try to draw it out. Clearly, she was not going to show any jealousy either.

The day after reaching these decisions, she changed her behavior during their daily phone call. She did not say "I love you" and neither did he. Two days later, she told him she was coming home and he said, "Good. I've missed you." This convinced her that her decision was the correct one and that she could live with it even if their relationship ended completely. After the break, I relayed the following message:

We are impressed with your decisions and that you put those into action so quickly. What you said today led the team to the idea that Jake may not be worthy of you and your affection.

I am not so sure I agree with them, because maybe what you see down deep inside Jake is really there. But if you can't passively draw it out, they may be right. I do wonder if you are willing to wait the years it might take?

"I am willing to wait weeks, maybe even a couple of months. But if I haven't by then, I won't wait years." According to the referral source, her sister-in-law, they were still together four months later.

DISCUSSION

With and without the formal use of trance, the therapy sessions at BFTC are designed to be hypnotic in character, altering the

habitual attitudes and modes of functioning so that carefully formulated hypnotic suggestions can evoke and utilize other patterns of association and potentials within the patient to implement certain therapeutic goals (Erickson, Rossi, and Rossi, 1976, p. 20).

Agatha Christie's Hercule Poirot described his method as listening to the witnesses and suspects until they told him what he wanted to know. From what Poirot heard he constructed a reality that led to a solution to the crime he was investigating. Similarly, during the interview phase of the session, the therapist needs to *listen* to the client because he or she will give the therapist the clues necessary to solving the problem. Every client carries the key to the solution: The therapist needs to know where to look. As the client talks, the therapist and the team listen for

(1) how much emphasis the client places on each of the 12 doors (see Chapter 2);

(2) which of the 12 doors is *not* mentioned;

(3) past successes the client mentions;

(4) things the client does that are good for him or her;

(5) descriptions of how the client deals with other people; and

(6) descriptions of what life will be like once the complaint is resolved.

Of course, the therapist needs to help the client focus on these areas and it is his job to prompt or elicit the clues necessary to building a therapeutic reality that leads to a solution.

While the therapist is taking a break to construct the closing therapeutic message, the client is left waiting in the therapy room. During this time the client wonders about what the therapist is going to say when he or she returns. The hypnotic purpose of the break is to promote the building of a "response attentiveness," which indicates that the client is really looking to the therapist for direction. This is *the* moment to introduce a therapeutic suggestion or a reframing (Erickson and Rossi, 1979).

To facilitate and promote the introduction of the therapeutic suggestion, the therapist begins the message with compliments or statements about what, in the therapist's opinion, the client is doing that is good for him or her. These comments may or may not have anything at all to do with the complaint. The purpose of the compliments is to build a "yes set" (Erickson et al., 1976; Erickson and Rossi, 1979; de Shazer, 1982a) that helps to get the client into a frame of mind to accept something new—the therapeutic task or directive. These directives, tasks, and suggestions are essentially designed to be posthypnotic suggestions and frequently are linked up with inevitable events which can serve as "triggers" that help the client do something different.

Although Erickson's "yes set" has been our descriptive metaphor for the client's accepting the intervention message or, more generally, any therapeutic suggestion, I am surprised that it has received little study by either hypnotherapists or family therapists. We have long asked ourselves, "What signs do clients give us that our intervention message has achieved at least minimal fit?" The simplest version of this question we were able to devise was: "If we assign a concrete task, what signs can we use to predict whether or not the client will perform the task?" Since many clients do not verbalize acceptance or non-acceptance, we decided to study nonverbal signs.

We had assumed that head nods would be the primary indicator, but our work and a study* we did suggests that simple head nods *alone* are insufficient to use as predictors of task compliance. However, if the client also actively repositions himself during or after the assignment of a task, then it is highly likely that he will perform the task. If eye contact is also maintained, the likelihood is further increased.

We have also found that if the client looks down or aside, avoiding eye contact, *and* sits with arms folded, then noncompliance can be most accurately predicted. Simply put, a responsive and receptive relationship has not been established and a therapeutic response is unlikely.

In the following chapters, the crystal ball technique and the principles behind it (see Chapter 4) have been used as major clues to how solutions develop.

---

*Three groups (first semester graduate students in clinical social work, fourth semester graduate students, and experienced therapists) were shown videotapes (without sound) taken during the intervention delivery segment of a group of sessions in which a task was assigned. First, they were asked to predict whether or not the client would perform the task and, second, they were asked to list what nonverbal behaviors they used to make that prediction. As expected, the therapists were most accurate in their predictions. For all three groups, however, the clusters of signs were associated with accurate predictions, but no one sign by itself was any more useful than any other.

Thanks to Jim Derks, formerly on BFTC's staff, Dave Pakenham and Laurie Ingraham, who were graduate students at the time (1981), for their assistance in this project.

6

THE CONSTRUCTION
OF PROBLEMS

GOALS STRUCTURE PROBLEMS

Once outside help is sought, the nature of the problem, as well as of potential remedies, becomes subject to redefinition by some outsider, such as a therapist. Any outside "intervention, then, may fundamentally shape what the trouble will become" (Emerson and Messinger, 1977, p.128). Therefore, goals are the "name of the game" in a solution-oriented therapy approach. Without goals, therapists and clients cannot know when the therapy has succeeded or failed. Without goals, therapists and clients tend to wander around in much the same circles the clients followed alone in the unsuccessful effort to solve their complaints. A simple rule: *Therapists need to know what not to do, and what the clients have been doing is usually the clearest illustration of what not to do.* However, since clients frequently have difficulty stating a goal, therapists need to construct problems in such a way that a goal or vision of the future emerges.

The principles behind the crystal ball technique (Erickson, 1954a; de Shazer, 1978a) can enable clients to know what their world might look like when the problem is solved. What one expects to happen colors or "determines" what is happening and what is going to happen. As long as one expects the same old thing to happen over and over again, it is likely that that expectation will be met. The expectation that a repeating pattern will repeat helps to develop expectations of continued repetitions (Berger, Cohen, and Zelditch, 1966). Change will occur as the conditions change in some way, but the process itself generates expectation-maintaining behaviors. Since expectations help to determine the nature of subsequent events, it seems clear that the behavior will change when the expectation changes.

When a goal is defined, the expectation of a different, more satisfactory future starts to develop and behavior changes in the present become possible. The future is made salient to the present; thus, the goal and the consequences of its achievement can "determine" or shape what happens next. Therefore, the question, "How are you going to know when the problem is solved?" is crucial to the development of a successful solution.

As the crystal ball technique illustrates, fit can be achieved quite easily when the goal and the consequences of its achievement are generated by the client rather than by the therapist. Clearly, it is the therapist's task to help generate and clarify these expectations since they do not arise when the complaint is generating itself.

Case Example: Slug-a-Bed*

A brief example will illustrate the connections between complaints, problem construction, potential solutions and goals, and tasks designed to reach the solution.

In the fourth session, Jan, a young, unemployed, professional woman, reported that she was feeling 10% better than she had felt prior to the first session. She constructed her complaint as a general malaise: Everything in her life was gray, no blacks and no whites. The therapist, who had been wondering about the direction the therapy was going to take without any concrete goals having been established in the first three sessions, asked Jan how she would know that things were better enough and how much better would things

*Carol Michalski, while a graduate student at BFTC, was the therapist in this case.

be at that point. Jan replied that 35% better would be all she
could expect without having a job. The therapist then asked
what Jan would be doing differently when she felt 35% better.

Jan then described her morning routine, which involved
staying in bed for two hours after the alarm went off at 8 or
9 a.m. She thought that when she felt 35% better she would
be like "normal people" and (1) get up between 6 and 8 a.m.
She also thought that she would then be able to (2) organize
her household better and keep up with the housework daily,
instead of putting it off until she had to do it, which meant
she cleaned once a month. She thought she lacked the will-
power to do these things she wanted to do, but that these
activities would make her feel better enough to (3) resume her
daily swimming.

The brief therapist now had enough information to design
a homework assignment built around the goals: (1) getting
up between 6 and 8 a.m. and (2) organizing the household and
doing her housework. In fact, both goals were things that Jan
viewed as "good for her" because they would allow her to
resume the swimming. After receiving a declaration of cooperation, the therapist told Jan about the "solution." This simply involved weaving the goals together. First, the therapist
honestly told Jan that she liked the idea of staying in bed for
two hours after the alarm and would not suggest changing
that. Instead, the therapist suggested, Jan should set her
alarm for 6 a.m. and then stay in bed. If, however, she was
still in bed at 8:01, then she had to do two hours of housework
immediately upon getting out of bed, even if she had to invent tasks. Since Jan was expecting to be told to take a cold
shower, she was relieved and pleased by this assignment.

The structure of this task is rather simple. If Jan gets out
of bed by 8:00, then she is doing something she wants and
needs to do but is not doing, and if she stays in bed until or
after 8:01, then she "punishes" herself by doing something she
wants to do and needs to do but is not doing. Both ways she
does something that is good for her. A bonus might even
develop: By getting up earlier she will have more time on her

hands and so might do the housework anyway. She might, in any case, use the extra time to go swimming.

Case Example: The Pseudo-bulimic*

At times, multiple or alternative goals can be useful in developing solutions. In the following case example, for instance, Maxine's behavior was originally defined by the family members as "strange." When it persisted in spite of Maxine's efforts to stop it, they defined it as a physical or medical concern, but this did not help. Then it was redefined as her "emotional problem" by a therapist, but again without a solution. Another therapist redefined it as a "family problem" (or rather, it was defined as the "young lady's problem" within a "family problem"). When the family failed to solve the "family problem" or the "young lady's problem," then the "family" was referred once again. Therefore, the complaint and the remedy became subject to multiple renegotiations, redefinitions – and finally, solution.

Maxine, 16, her sister Sally, 17, and their parents came for therapy because Maxine vomited after each and every meal. Maxine and the rest of the family thought she needed to understand "why" she vomited so that she could stop. At first the vomiting had been deliberate and forced, but when she stopped the behavior she found, to her surprise, that she continued to vomit automatically or involuntarily. The therapist asked her what she would be doing differently when she stopped vomiting and she replied that she would then be able to eat what she wanted to eat rather than restricting herself to what she thought would stay down. She also thought that her sister would stop teasing her or would at least tease less. She went on to describe (and show during the session) other conflicts and difficulties between her sister (who was seen by the family as wearing a white hat) and herself. The whole family agreed that Maxine was "somehow different" from the

---

*John H. Weakland was a guest member of the team for the second session of this case.

rest, and they all agreed that it was important to her to be seen as different, even though the other family members did not like it.

The vomiting was sort of secret, in that neither of the parents nor Sally knew for sure if and when she did it. There was, as far as could be determined, no active interactional pattern surrounding the vomiting, (no first A, then B, then vomit, then C, then D pattern was reported as having ever occurred). Mother and father checked once a week or so to find out if she was still vomiting and her sister teased her about it (and anything else). The parents seemed to work well together as a team and were doing everything they could think of to get help for their daughter. They were concerned but saw themselves as helpless in the face of this deviance. The therapist asked the family members to rank order themselves on the question, "Who is most upset by this problem?" Each of the four gave a different ranking. Mother was ranked first by father, mother and Maxine ranked Maxine first, and her sister ranked father first.

The team saw this ranking as rather congruent with their view: Everybody in the family seemed equally concerned and equally unconcerned. These observations ruled out certain problem constructions:

(1) Since there was so little interaction around the complaint, it would be hard to design the problem around the notion that the vomiting was "holding the family together" or that the vomiting was Maxine's sacrifice for the family.

(2) Since the parents were not an over/underinvolved set, the problem could not be designed in such a way that the underinvolved one became more involved in order to prompt solution.

(3) Since the parents clearly seemed to be functioning well as a team, and the two girls were behaving in more or less age-appropriate ways and were successful at school, designing the problem around the need to put the parents in charge as parents would not "fit" for the

family because the girls had reached the age of growing independence and self-sufficiency.

A therapist might accept Maxine's definition (automatic
vomiting) and the suggested solution (finding out "why") if
he, too, saw that as a solution (that is, if they shared the same
map). But the family and the previous therapists had already
tried that! Nonetheless, the therapist spent some time unsuccessfully exploring "why" with Maxine and her family since
they seemed convinced this was a necessary step (or, at least,
they thought this would interest the therapist). However,
the problem needed to be defined differently so that a solution could be found.

The complaint was defined as an aberration beyond the
family's or Maxine's control *and* as belonging solely to Maxine. The team, therefore, decided to see Maxine alone. The
rest of the family was not seen again. (If mother had been
ranked as the most upset by the family, a different problem
might have been constructed and the solution might have involved seeing mother alone.) The team knew of some ways
to define the problem and, therefore, some potential solutions
that would stop the vomiting without Maxine's precondition
of understanding "why" she vomited. The sessions had confirmed that Maxine was doing things well within the normal
range for her age: going to school, dating, working part-time,
participating in sports, etc. For two sessions, the therapist
and the team attempted to solve the problem using the frame
that "she was being different" but in a way that was not good
for her. They agreed with her that being different was valuable and she should continue to be different. In the short run
she might need to continue to vomit until she found a different way to be different, a way that was at least not bad for
her.

However, this approach did not prompt her to invent a new
way to be different to solve the problem. It did not fit because
Maxine had defined herself as a "helpless victim of the vomiting." The vomiting was "spontaneous" and the "cure" also
needed to be spontaneous as far as she was concerned. There-

fore, the problem needed to be reconstructed. Fortunately, Maxine had provided the team with some other goals, one of which included changing her relationship with her sister.

In the third session with Maxine, the therapist asked her if she would do what he told her to do to stop the vomiting even if she did not know why she had vomited or why he was telling her to do whatever he told her to do. He assured her that the solution would be good for her and it would not be immoral, illegal, dangerous, or difficult, though it might be fattening since she would no longer vomit. Since Maxine wanted to stop (she placed herself at nine on a scale from one to ten rating how much she wanted to quit), she agreed.

The team decided that a fit could be achieved if Maxine became the helpless victim of an intervention. To further increase the fit, the therapist became the helpless victim of the team behind the mirror. This is only a minor change in the normal routine; usually the team behind the mirror is in charge of designing the interventions and the therapist in the room has only limited "veto" power.

Maxine had said that one way she would know the problem was solved was when there was a change in her relationship with her sister. Therefore, the therapist and the team reconstructed the problem as one between the two girls – one teasing and baiting, the other reacting involuntarily with defensiveness and withdrawal – which could be solved by some different behavior.

The therapist told Maxine that he was sure she would not like the "cure," but she had agreed to follow orders. He was exceedingly reluctant to tell her what the "cure" was, because he thought it was horrible, but since the rule was that he had to do what the team told him to do, he was going to tell her in spite of his reluctance. He also felt obligated to tell her since it would work. Maxine wondered if it might embarrass her. He was afraid it might. Would that stop her from doing what she had agreed to do? Maxine reassured him that it would not. He then told her the "cure": From now on, if she vomited, she needed to give her sister five one-dollar bills within 24 hours without offering any explanation and to get a receipt for the money. Maxine appeared puzzled and thought this behavior would make her sister think she was really crazy. However, she had agreed to do what she was told. By means of this task and the blind faith agreement, the involuntary vomiting had again become voluntary. As it turned out, *fit* was achieved by tying the problem and intervention design to the helpless victim frame and by attaching the task to the secondary goal. In the following session, she brought in two receipts gathered in 14 days. She knew now why she had stopped vomiting—it had become expensive—and why the therapist had given her that specific assignment. She changed her (now voluntary) vomiting behavior in order to change her (now involuntary and paying) relationship with her sister. She no longer cared about why she used to vomit, but was only concerned with how to make sure she did not ever again have to pay her sister for the privilege.

The therapist suggested that since she did not know "why" she had vomited in the first place, she might find herself vomiting more in the coming weeks. Maxine rejected this and subsequently proved the therapist wrong. In the final session five weeks later, Maxine reported that she had not had to pay her sister any more money, and there was less teasing and less conflict between them. The old involuntary behaviors had been replaced by new, voluntary behaviors that were not withdrawal.

Case Example: Three Is No Fluke*

At times, when the client's goal is poorly described or too large, the therapist can help to promote solution by clearly offering some minimal measures of change.

Mr. Able, 49, came to therapy because he had been having erectile difficulties for over a year. He came to see me as a result of reading a newspaper article in which my work was

*Scott Fraser was a guest member of the team for the first session of this case.

described as "weird and effective." Of course, with this expectation of the unorthodox, the therapist would be hard pressed to come up with an intervention as weird as the client might expect! This therapy, he thought, would give him the "kick in the pants" he needed. He described the marital relationship as solid but getting ragged around the edges because of the prolonged absence of sexual intercourse. Although sex had never been frequent in their marriage (averaging once a month), this time the interval had become too long for both him and his wife. In fact, the most recent attempt had been three months earlier and it ended with his wife crying.

After straightforward attempts to define a measurable goal for therapy, I asked him, "How are you going to know when you and your wife have successfully had sex three, or four, or five times that that is no fluke?" Mr. Able could not answer that question with anything specific, beyond that he and his wife would get along better, and the interview went on. My question, "How are you going to know . . . it's no fluke?" is based on the presupposition that the desired change will happen; it is not a question of *if* they will have successful sex, but *when* they will have successful sex. Furthermore, the question makes the suggestion that three or four or five successes would mean that the problem is solved, it is no fluke, and a measurable goal is established.

Mr. Able went on to describe a concern he had about his concentration at work. He found himself daydreaming and procrastinating, using long-range projects to interfere with short-range projects, and thereby accomplishing neither. Somehow and in some way, he saw the two complaints as interconnected. The exact connection was not clear to him, nor could he make it clear to the therapist and team, despite great effort.

As part of the intervention message, I remarked that the team and I were also not sure about the connection between the lack of concentration and the lack of sex; in fact, the team was "not sure what solution would solve which problem." In the client's frame there was a connection between the two concerns; therefore, the team began a reframing in which the solutions might also be connected in some way. Regarding the sexual complaint, I said, "Most sex therapists would suggest that you do not try to have sex." This phrasing allows the therapist to avoid giving the instruction not to have sex or the message not even to try. The implication here is that having successful sex is certainly not *trying* — it is *succeeding*. A kind of focus or rapport between therapist and client develops from these types of questions and the implicit messages about change and solution.

The question "How would you know it was no fluke?" makes the presupposition that the client will respond with cooperating behavior. Of course, any response the client makes helps to define his own way of being "cooperative," and thus the therapist retains a flexible range within which to fit his responses to the client's responses. This is similar to Erickson's arm levitation approach. Simply, Erickson would not demand that the subject "unconsciously lift up your left arm," because if the client did not, then the receptivity would not be promoted and the trance would lose some, if not most, of its effectiveness. Rather, Erickson might approach it this way, "I don't know if your right arm or your left arm is going to lift up toward your face, or if your right arm or your left arm is going to press down, or both are going to remain the same; lifting up or pressing down or remaining the same is not important; what is important is that you, pay attention to whatever feelings develop in either arm." If the right arm should lift up, then Erickson could define this as cooperation and go on from there, encouraging the levitation. If neither lifted or neither pressed down, Erickson could define that as cooperation and continue the induction.

In Mr. Able's case, (a) trying, (b) not trying, and (c) succeeding were all covered, as was (d) trying and failing. If he had tried and failed, the therapist's "when" stance would still be valid. The same would be true if he had not tried. A simple rule might be proposed here: Since the client comes to the therapist wanting change, a most useful stance for the therapist to take is that change is inevitable. Consequently, the therapist can frame his questions about changing as "when" questions rather than "if" questions.

At the second session, before I finished my opening question, Mr. Able stated, "We had sex three times just to prove it was no fluke." He seemed to have no direct awareness of the relationship between his statement and the question from the week before. I did not question him about this, preferring to leave the possible amnesia intact. In this way the client can rightfully take full credit for the change. After the previous session, he had talked to his wife at some length about having come to therapy and about his renewed optimism about eventually solving the problem. This was far different from their usual talks dealing with the frustration of their sex life. We can speculate that the first session had allowed or prompted this different conversation because Mr. and Mrs. Able no longer felt pressure to do anything to solve the problem. After all, an "expert" had told him not to try. For the first time, he also told his wife about the procrastination at work. The evening after this talk, the first of the sexual episodes "just sort of happened." Neither he nor his wife really initiated this one or the other two (meaning, perhaps, that he did not try!). My response was to investigate how they got together for sex without either of them really initiating it, rather than focusing on the change.

Mr. Able also reported some increase in his ability to concentrate. He had finished the long-range planning project and now had no excuse for not working on short-term projects. The team asked him to watch how he stopped procrastinating and got himself back to the work at hand. Since clients tend to report and show more concern about how something starts than about how it ends, this message is an attempt to shift his focus. Of course, there is a global suggestion in this message that the procrastination will stop, i.e., the problem will be solved.

Two weeks later, the client continued to report successful sex, seven times within this two-week period. This was the highest frequency in their marriage – as far as he could remember. I was not surprised that they had continued to have sex without either of them initiating it. Mr. Able was unsure about how he had turned off his daydreaming, but he had come to the realization that the trouble at work was due to boredom. Once he realized that, daydreaming ceased. The therapist and team worried about a "relapse" in either area.

In this case, as in many cases, the "new frame" is only suggested in various ways. Mr. Able's view of the world included the idea that "problems" happened and that a person needed to *do* something in order to solve problems. In fact, he came to therapy – in his words – to get a "kick in the pants" toward doing something to solve the sexual problem. The "fluke" question and subsequent events opened up a new frame in which good things just "happened" and problems could be solved by "not doing" rather than trying harder.

CONCLUSION

Constructing problems in ways which lead to potential solution is essential. Without this, the therapist can easily join the client on a circular pathway that leads from problem to problem – not to solution. When clients cannot define their goals in such a way that a solution can evolve, this becomes the therapist's job. Of course, the client needs to agree with these goals, and accomplishing them needs to be a solution to the complaint.

7

KEEP IT SIMPLE

WHOLISM

In the search for solutions to clinical problems, the concept of wholism stands out as a useful lens to use when looking at the complexities involved. Simply stated, "systems theory" as applied to human systems and their difficulties suggests that families (or any group of people with a history and a future) are not just an aggregate of individuals. Rather, a human system is more than the sum of its parts. It is not only the individuals included in the description but also the relationships between and among those individuals. Thus, a systems view necessitates a certain complexity. However, since a system is a whole, "every part of a system is so related to its fellow parts that change in one part will cause a change in all of them and in the total system" (Watzlawick et al., 1967, p. 123). This allows us to, on the one hand, minimize, and on the other, utilize the complexity so that solutions can be found. Only a fit is necessary; otherwise the solutions, to be effective, might need to match a reality as complex as the human system plus the systemic problem.

For our purposes, "problems" can be defined as those things clients complain about to therapists and about which the therapists and the clients can do something. If the complaint is something they cannot do anything about, then the complaint is not a problem—no matter how painful and severe it may be. Of course, to therapists some of the things clients complain about may seem trivial and just a part of life and some of the things clients do not complain about may seem worthy of complaint. Nonetheless, the "complaint" is a problem as long as client and therapist can do something about it.

The "system" under consideration can be defined as client-plus-complaint-plus-therapist. Just as the "client" may be a family or a couple or an individual, the "therapist" may also include a team behind the mirror and a videotape machine, etc. When a team approach to therapy is under consideration, the "system" includes: (1) the client, (2) the complaint, (3) the therapist, (4) the setting (mirror and VTR), (5) the team behind the mirror, and (6) the interactional relationships between and among these elements. In accordance with the concept of wholism, change in the therapeutic system might be punctuated as starting anywhere in the system (de Shazer and Molnar, 1984a). For example, the team might need to change its membership and/or its view of things before the solution can be found, the apparent relationship between the therapist and the rest of the team may need to change in some way, or the team may need to change who is filling the role of therapist in the room, etc. Although the therapeutic system with a team is more complex than the client-complaint-therapist version, the variety of options available for initiating change and thus solving problems outweighs the possible confusions.

Clients' complaints may take the form of a wife or husband complaining about the marriage, or a parent or parents complaining about their child or children. Sometimes, during the course of therapy, only one person shows up for the appointment when the therapist was expecting more. If it were not for the concept of wholism, having just "part" of the client system might seem to be a handicap in finding a solution. However, the person who comes to the appointment is frequently the one with the most pressing complaint and, therefore, the one who wants to work with the therapist toward getting something different to happen within the troublesome area. As Weakland (1983) puts it:

In simplest terms, [the interactional view] proposes that if interaction between members of a social system is seen as the primary shaper and determinant of ongoing behavior, it then follows that alteration of the behavior of any one member of a system of interaction – particularly a family, as the most ubiquitous, encompassing and enduring kind of system – must lead to a related alteration in the behavior of other members of the system (p. 2).

The idea that a system is more than the sum of its parts can be problematic for systemic therapists (and other "family therapists"), since their unit of description is the family group. For instance, Ferrier (1984) discovered that "it has not been clear whether the systemic approach developed by the Milan Associates is susceptible to adaptation to work with these abbreviated families" (i.e., single-parent families, particularly those with very young children). Fortunately, Ferrier found that "not only is it possible to make this adaptation, but that it [the techniques and methods] can be effective within a fairly brief time." Ferrier concludes that even though it is "easier" and perhaps more efficient to work with the group that lives together, "it may well be more efficient in the long run, in those cases where only one or a few members are readily available, to accept whatever unit comes as information about the system and to proceed from there." This is close to the position suggested here: Solving the problem is the clinical task.

Szapocznik, Kurtines, Foote, Perez-Vidal, and Hervis (1983) compared "conjoint" family therapy and "one person" family therapy (sessions with just the "identified patient"), using a structuralist approach. They found that "both conditions were equally effective in improving family functioning and reducing symptomatology in the IP at termination" (p. 898). Interestingly, one-person family therapy was found to be "somewhat more effective" in maintaining continued improvement in the IP's symptoms. Since the population in this study was limited to drug abusers and their families, we might speculate that the *more currently important* system was the drug-oriented peer network. It is possible that the one-person format is more effective in promoting changes in the peer system.

The idea that the whole family needs to be involved in the therapy stems from the view held by some therapists that the family is the patient and, therefore, it is not therapeutic to see only some members of the family. However, as Szapocznik et al. show, the assumption behind this perspective is questionable.

Solving clients' complaints need not, and frequently does not, involve seeing the whole family. Watzlawick and Coyne (1980) describe a case in which the participants in the sessions complained about how they had not dealt well with father's predicament–recovery from a stroke. They describe this therapy as "treating the depressed patient only through contact with his family" (p.17). However, the "problem" was not Mr. B's depression; rather, it was the complaints of the other family members. Therapy created a solution to those complaints. The effects upon Mr. B provide a good illustration of how one part of a system changes as a result of changes in other parts of the system, once again suggesting that the *problem*, rather than either an individual or a family, is the patient.

In fact, Coyne (1984) goes further and suggests that there are good "reasons for not interviewing both members of a couple with a depressed person together, at least initially" (p. 55). For instance, the nondepressed spouse may be on the way out of the marriage and is just waiting for the depressed person to improve enough to handle a divorce. Or, each spouse may have some magical ideas about what the marriage is going to be like or should be like once the depressed partner is better. Furthermore, it can be easier "to get clear information about key incidents from one in the absence of the other. Together, they tend to lapse into a pattern of inhibition and withdrawal or, alternatively, emotional outbursts, characterological criticisms and accusations" (p. 56). Of course, this sort of information may be relevant, but a report from each separately is just as useful in finding a solution to the problem.

*Case Example: Tit for Tat**

This case illustrates the application of the systemic concept of wholism to the solution of a marital difficulty which was presented by the wife when she came to therapy. At no time was the husband included in the therapy; in fact, he was not invited. The changes in the husband's behavior can be seen as a result of the differences in the wife's behavior and in how she framed the situation.

Mrs. Johns was feeling desperate and in a panic about her marriage. She complained that her husband frequently went out at night without her, then stayed out as late as 4:30 a.m. or did not come home at all. He told her he was going out with his single, male friend, and she believed him. Whenever she expressed her resentment, her huband comforted her about their relationship and assured her that there was nothing to worry about. Consequently, she continued to accept his going out and even kissed him good-bye and wished him a "good time," because she felt he would go out anyway, no matter what she said or did.

Meanwhile, she stayed at home and suffered stomach pains, diarrhea, depression, crying bouts, headaches, and recently thoughts of suicide, which she rejected because of their two children, aged four and six. However, her priorities were clear: She wanted this particular marriage and was willing to do almost anything to make it work.

She had tried talking to him about it; she had tried passively accepting it; then she had talked to him some more. Since nagging and suffering had not worked to keep him home, she now wanted to know what to do to change things. She clearly saw that any changes to be made were hers, since he

---

*Further explication of this case material appears in de Shazer and Berg, 1984.

thought everything was OK. If she could not stop his going out, then she wanted to be able to accept his going out without becoming emotionally upset. She saw that as part of her job as "wife" and as the price she had to pay for this marriage. Mrs. Johns had repeatedly modified her behavior in hopes of modifying his behavior, which indicated that she would probably be willing to try more new behaviors – to do something different.

Mr. Johns was a detective, and detectives usually love mysteries. This fact, along with the fact that he did not know his wife was coming to therapy, prompted the whole design for solving the problem.

The therapist complimented Mrs. Johns on her fairness and her patience in this trying situation and also complimented her on having tried everything she could think of to solve the problem. However, it seemed she had not been mysterious enough. Every marriage needs some mystery, and since Mrs. Johns described herself as an open book, the therapist suspected that her detective husband, who needed more than the average amount of mystery, was out of a job.

The therapist then listed a variety of things Mrs. Johns might do to make things mysterious, such as getting all dressed up and going out before he left the house without telling him where she was going or not being at home when he got there at 4:30 in the morning without leaving word where she was.

She was cautioned to not do too much too quickly, but she might want to just think about these sort of things so that she had a plan ready. Mrs. Johns thought the suggestions were good ones and recognized that they were the opposite of what she had been doing.

At the start of the second session, Mrs. Johns said, "I suppose, in a sense, I've reached my goal. My husband did not go out this week!" For the first time in two years, a week had gone by without his going out alone. Since she now had a plan, she felt in control of her situation. On the third evening after the previous session, Mrs. Johns went out by herself (tit for tat), returning about 1:00 a.m. He was there waiting, but they did not talk about it at all.

Although her behavior might not have stopped him from going out, it did have that effect that week (at least as she punctuated it). Therefore, she had at least the illusion of controlling his behavior by taking more control of hers. This successful change was enough to breed further confidence, which prompted further changes and consequent solution to the problem.

The therapist complimented her on what she had done differently and on what she planned to do on future evenings when Mr. Johns went out alone and she did not want him to. The therapist also suggested that she urge him to go out one night, on his night off, and to insist that he stay out until one or two o'clock. Mrs. Johns particularly liked this idea since she felt it would shock him as much as it shocked her.

In the final session, Mrs. Johns reported that everything was just fine. She had used the therapist's ideas and found out that they worked. In the first week after the previous session, Mr. Johns had gone out, and she knew far enough in advance to make plans. She hired a baby-sitter, went shopping, and rented a motel room. When she returned home at 5:00 a.m. he was there. He had returned at two. He never asked her where she went or what she had done, and she had not volunteered the information. However, he did not go out again.

Four weeks later, he asked her permission to go out. (He had never before asked.) She answered, "You have to do what you feel you want to do." He decided to go out and invited her to spend the evening with his friend's girlfriend. "I decided that wouldn't work because then he'd know exactly where I was and what I was doing, so I said, 'No, I've already made plans to go out.'" Several hours later he said, "Let's both cancel our plans and spend the evening together." That was what they did. The change in his behavior was exactly what she wanted to have happen and, therefore, the goal of therapy was met.

Case Example: Creating a Thirst for Change

This case example again illustrates treatment influenced by the principle of wholism. The therapist decided that no good purpose would be served by mother's dragging in her reluctant daughter or disinterested husband.

Mrs. Webster came to therapy complaining that Mr. Webster would not join her and neither would her daughter Colleen, age 16, who was, after all, the trouble. She and Mr. Webster had disagreed about how to handle Colleen for years. Now things were getting out of hand and Mr. Webster still could not see the need for help because he thought, "she'll grow out of it." Mrs. Webster decided to come for therapy after reading about our "radical" approach in the local newspaper. She really wanted to bring her daughter in for therapy, but she knew her daughter would not come because Mr. Webster would side with her against coming.

Colleen's troublesome behavior, as described by Mrs. Webster, included: not going to classes, always sleeping late and missing the school bus; getting poor to awful grades; leaving clothes and garbage scattered around the house; not doing her assigned chores; harassing the four younger children; being disagreeable; going out when grounded; lying; stealing; and smoking in her room. She reported that Colleen felt that the only thing wrong was that she (mother) was unfair and overdemanding. Mother thought Colleen needed to realize these were her problems and that Colleen needed to be in therapy to solve them.

The team gave Mrs. Webster the following message:

> We are impressed with your concern about Colleen's going to hell in a handbasket and your decision to act before things get so critical that the bottom falls out. Sometimes it is hard to know when to act, when to, do something different, when there's chaos and confusion. In spite of this, you were able to clearly describe your situation and, therefore, we have a beginning picture or a start toward getting a handle on it.
>
> We are sorry that we don't have anything "radical" to suggest, tonight, although we well may in the future. We do, however, suggest that you keep your coming here a secret—if she doesn't already know.

In order to be able to help her straighten around, you need to get her into a position where she is thirsty enough so that, when you lead her to water, she'll have to drink.

We suggest you give some serious thought to how you are going to turn the tables on her, how you can start to get her thirsty.

Mrs. Webster realized that we did not want her to drag Colleen in with her, but agreed that if Colleen were given some trouble, then she might want to come in.

At the time of this first session, Mrs. Webster had so many complaints that she was unable to focus on one deserving our initial attention. So, although the complaints were rather specific, none of them led to a goal specific enough to be useful. She wanted Colleen to straighten up totally and was unable to accept a small change as a sign of progress. Therefore, the team decided on a "think task" which might help Mrs. Webster focus on something specific in the second session. The team also was attempting to redefine the situation as one about which Mrs. Webster herself could *do something other than complain*.

In the second session, mother reported that Colleen's behavior had gone from bad to worse. This prompted Mrs. Webster to think about dropping out of college for the time being in order to "baby-sit" Colleen. This was the only alternative Mrs. Webster could imagine. However, she did not want to do this and hoped we had something else in mind. The therapist assured her that he had something much smaller in mind.

The therapist agreed that Mrs. Webster's dropping out of college well might work to get Colleen up on time and off to school; however, it was the kind of sacrifice that Colleen had seen her mother make before. The following statement was made:

We think that since you never know what to expect from Colleen, but she knows what to expect from you, this needs to change. We think you need to do things that Colleen can't expect you to do which will make her thirsty enough to change.

The therapist then told a story about a mother who solved a morning difficulty. What she did was to sneak into her daughter's room after she was sleeping and set the alarm for two hours earlier than normal. The next day daughter bitched, but mother maintained her silence. The following night, she reset it for three hours later than normal. Again the daughter bitched. The third night mother did not change the alarm, and the daughter got up on time the next day and most days thereafter.

The therapist told another story about a mother who was angry at her daughter for not picking up dirty clothes, etc. One day, while the daughter was gone, mother stole all her makeup. The mother did not mention picking up dirty clothes. The daughter complained a lot about the missing makeup. A few days later, when the clothes were still not picked up, mother stole all of her daughter's left shoes. When daughter complained, mother simply told her that she knew what she needed to do to earn her shoes back. Daughter not only picked up dirty clothes, but did some other chores. Mother, knowing the girl had an "important date," gave her the worst left shoe. Daughter did not complain and chores were no longer an issue.

Mrs. Webster chuckled throughout these true stories and clearly had figured out the kind of things we were suggesting. In the following weeks, she used some of these techniques and invented some of her own.

In the final session, Mrs. Webster reported that the changes in Colleen's behavior had spread from home to the school. She even brought homework home for the first time in two years. She was going to classes regularly and doing most of her chores on time. Even Mr. Webster had remarked about these changes, saying, "See, I told you she'd grow out of it." Mrs. Webster did not tell him about her therapy and how she got her daughter thirsty enough.

Case Example: The Retired SOB*

This case illustrates how deliberate changes made by one person can affect not only the marital system but also a larger surrounding system. The husband was disinvited because the complaints seemed more readily solvable through working just with the wife.

Two months prior to the initial appointment, Mr. C, 72, who was a nursing home resident, had had an unexplained fall which left him very frightened and with some continuing pain. The doctors concluded that there was no physiological reason for his not having recovered to his previous level of functioning. His condition became increasingly worse, he lost 21 pounds, refused to get out of bed, lost interest in former activities, became irritable, rejected the ministrations of the nursing home staff, and, in particular, demanded the constant presence of his wife.

Prior to this, Mrs. C, who still worked full-time, would visit her husband in the evenings and on weekends. On those rare occasions when she could not visit, he had accepted this, as long as he had been told in advance.

When Mr. C first became demanding after his fall, Mrs. C had complied with his wishes, thinking that this would speed her husband's recovery. Instead he seemed to get progressively worse. The more she tried to please him, the more demanding and irritable he became. At this point she felt totally trapped. If she did not visit daily and do all the things Mr. C demanded, he not only became angry with her but also made trouble for the staff. The staff, in turn, complained to her and made her feel guilty. Since she was about to retire and was afraid her husband would demand her presence even during the day, she agreed to some therapy.

Mr. and Mrs. C met at BFTC for the first session. Mr. C had been brought by a nursing home van since he was in a wheelchair. From the moment he was wheeled in the door, he appeared to be extremely angry. He denied having been told

*Further explication of this case material appears in de Shazer and Lipchik, 1984.

the purpose of the meeting, and when he was informed of it, he said, "Are things that bad?" He rejected all of the therapist's attempts to establish rapport and removed his hearing aid or wheeled himself away from the group when he did not like what he heard.

Behind the screen, it seemed clear that Mr. C was a tough old SOB who was discouraged and angry about his helplessness and dependence. When this idea was phoned in and relayed to him by the therapist, he became more animated than at any other time in the session. He denied being a tough SOB any longer, removed the hearing aid, and wheeled himself away. Mrs. C, however, agreed that she had seen him as being a tough old SOB prior to the fall. The team then speculated that although Mr. C made demands, Mrs. C's compliance made him angry and confirmed his fears of being terminally ill. The team gave the couple the following message:

> Jonathan, we are very impressed with how difficult it must be for you to have to put up with all this, and not be with Judith all the time, but despite all that, you show a lot of spirit. You still look like a man who knows what he wants and you haven't given up. You still have a lot of spirit.
>
> We are also impressed that after 42 years of marriage you still care for your wife so much.
>
> Judith, we are also struck with your efforts to make Jonathan happy and still have a life of your own. Most wives would not be nearly as caring and loyal as you are.
>
> We think you are both in a difficult situation, and the fact that you, Judith, are trying the best you can for *both* of you—not only yourself—is very impressive. Many women would not be so unselfish.

An appointment was then made for just Mrs. C. The team thought it would be more useful to work with her alone and to construct with her a problem she could do something about.

Mrs. C's attitude had changed somewhat when she returned the following week. She appeared less helpless and spoke of becoming tougher, even though she commented, "That is not my nature." She feared Mr. C's changed behavior and steady decline were either a sign that the doctors were missing something and he was sicker than they thought or evidence that he had given up. She described dreading her visits with him not only because he was so demanding, but also because the nursing home staff was so irritated with her for not making him behave better.

The therapist suggested that before Mr. C could give her more freedom, he would have to feel better about himself and become more independent. Mr. C needed a challenge, such as proving he could still do something for his wife like he used to. It was suggested that Mrs. C might have to sacrifice some of her helpful ways and even pretend to be sick, helpless, or dependent in order to get Mr. C to help her.

One week later, Mrs. C reported that her husband had had a very good week. For the first time in months he was hungry and eating solid food again. He had also agreed to go back to physical therapy and was working hard to regain his mobility. She did not really know how to account for these changes. However, she did describe a change in her attitude and behavior. She reported that she had stopped giving in to him so much. When he did not want to sit in the dining room with her while she had some coffee, she told him to go back to his room alone, where she would join him later. He did. She had decided that it was time to stop treating him like he was hopelessly ill and to stand up to him again, as she had in the past. Her husband seemed a little surprised at her behavior this week, but was not complaining too much about it.

Essentially, the remaining two sessions were devoted to promoting these changes and worrying about a relapse that never happened.

After Mr. C's fall, Mrs. C and the staff had operated within a frame which described their giving in to Mr. C's demands as "helpful," which implied that Mr. C was "helpless," no longer strong, and therefore no longer independent. The more they tried to be helpful, the more Mr. C labeled himself as "helpless," since this confirmed his frame, which was built on his fears and his temporarily weakened physical condition. Thus, he stopped eating and confined himself to his bed to die. The less he ate and the less he moved, the weaker he got; the more "helpful" people became, the more completely his worst fears were confirmed.

The above is an example of how two labels, "helpless" and "helpful," can interact to the detriment of all. The behaviors falling under each label tend to confirm the other label and to contribute to the development of a mutually escalating pattern.

CONCLUSION

The approach in all three cases used the principle of systemic wholism as a foundation. In each case, one person in the family deliberately made some changes in behavior that prompted changes in other family members and even in larger systems. "Tit for tat" has developed as a shorthand or code name for this approach, since that is exactly what is involved. The clients started to respond in kind to the complaint-provoking behaviors of others, rather than continuing to play the victim. Since the others could no longer predict what was going to happen next, they started to behave in ways that would eliminate or minimize the retaliatory actions of the complainant.

In each case, fit was achieved because both therapists and clients constructed the problem in such a way that the individual person could do something to solve the problem in the larger interactional systems. This framing of the situation fit the clients' world view and thus solution was reached.

8

SKELETON KEYS

Most of the writing on brief therapy, systemic therapy, and strategic therapy has focused on tailor-made interventions designed for idiosyncratic situations. However, this chapter and Chapter 9 describe interventions that have been found useful with a wide variety of difficult situations. Coincidentally with our work, Selvini-Palazzoli and Prata (1980) invented an invariant prescription which they use across the board with families ("hopeless cases"). They suggest that in this prescription they have "found the springboard to get to the heart of the problem. Furthermore, this was *without* considering a lot of details that could get us off the track" (emphasis added). Both their prescription (which follows a formula) and our "formula tasks" (each of which are standardized) suggest something about the nature of therapeutic intervention and change which has not been clearly described before: Interventions can initiate change without the therapist's first understanding, in any detail, what has been going on.

But what is going on here? Both the BFTC team and the Milan team seem to think that the therapist need not know many details of the complaint in order to at least initiate the solution of the problem. The interventions, therefore, need only prompt the initiation of some *new* behavior patterns. The exact nature of the trouble does not seem important to effectively generating solutions, because the intervention needs only to fit. Just a skeleton key is called for, not the one-and-only key designed to specifically match the specific lock.

WRITE, READ, AND BURN

I developed the first of what we now call "formula interventions" for a specific case in 1969. A young woman had broken up with her boyfriend, much against her will. For months after the breakup she had obsessed about this, dreamt about this, and blamed herself – trying to figure out what she had done wrong. She remembered the good things that had happened and she remembered the bad, mainly the unreasonable and unexpected end to a relationship she thought was heading toward marriage. At the time of the first session, these thoughts had progressed to nightmares. She thought about him all day – and all night too.

After explaining to her that it was normal to have thought a lot about these things and that she needed to think about these things in order to get over the hurt and pain, I gave her the following task as a way of concentrating her efforts so that she could get on with life.

(1) She was to find a comfortable place in which she could spend one quiet hour by herself each day at the same time. She was to spend at least one hour, but no more than an hour and a half, every day working on concentrating her efforts by:

(2) on odd numbered days, writing down all her good and bad memories about her ex-boyfriend. She was to write for the whole period, but no more than one and a half hours, even if this meant writing the same five sentences over and over. Then,

(3) on even numbered days, she was to read the previous day's notes and then burn them.

(4) If these unwanted thoughts came to her at other, unscheduled times, she was to either say to herself, "I have other things to think about now; I'll think about this at my regular time," or make a note to remind herself to concentrate on these thoughts during the regular time.

Within three days the nightmares stopped, and the "obsessive thoughts" stopped by the fifth day. Then she discontinued the write-read-burn task because she had better things to do.

The write-read-burn ritual needs to be delivered with confidence by the therapist because the switch from thinking about something to writing about the same thing and then burning it might seem a rather improbable solution to some clients. Over the years, clients have explained how this works:

(1) it objectifies their concerns or makes them more concrete;
(2) not thinking the troublesome thoughts is easier because there is a scheduled time for this kind of thinking;
(3) since the "bad" thoughts are no longer forbidden, thinking about other things becomes easier;
(4) the troubles literally go up in smoke; and
(5) the client realizes that he or she has "better things to do."

This formula is useful when the client complains of "obsessive thoughts" or "depressing thoughts." Most frequently, clients write no more than three times before they find better things to do and the troublesome thoughts are gone. Sometimes, people turn these notes into diaries. The therapist might suggest that if they cannot bring themselves to burn these notes, then they need to start a new diary when the unwanted thoughts have been gone for a week or two. In fact, the task can be drastically modified and still be effective. Recently, a man going through an unwanted divorce complained of thinking so much about it that it was interfering with his work. He was given the write-read-burn task. In the following session, three weeks later, he reported having his thoughts well under control, which he did by following only the fourth step in the ritual: scheduling a time for the next day. Then, on the next day he would keep himself so busy that he did not have time to think. After five or six days he no longer found even this to be necessary.

THE STRUCTURED FIGHT TASK

In 1974 I invented the "structured fight" task to fit a particular couple's troublesome situation, with some surprising results (de Shazer, 1977). This formula has been found useful in the process of promoting solution when both people complain about their arguments or fights. The ritual involves these steps:

(1) Toss a coin to decide who goes first.
(2) The winner gets to bitch for 10 uninterrupted minutes.
(3) Then the other person gets a 10-minute turn.
(4) Then there needs to be 10 minutes of silence before another round is started with a coin toss.

This intervention is specifically designed to fit situations in which both partners simultaneously complain about fights or arguments that seem never to settle anything. It is not useful in finding solutions for the wider range of complaints clients bring to therapists, i.e., if only one of the spouses is complaining about the arguments. However, the transferability of these two "formula tasks" gave us the idea that properly constructed tasks could be used again and again with little modification in a variety of similar cases. The same solution can be used over and over again without regard to the specific details of the complaint.

"DO SOMETHING DIFFERENT"

The "do something different" task was invented in 1978 to fit one specific case. The results the family reported prompted us to develop a formula version for other similar cases. The criteria for use of this formula were quickly recognized: One person is complaining about the behavior of another person and, having tried "everything," has become stuck reacting in the same way over and over while the troublesome behavior continues. The wording for the task has become quite standardized. In this case the message is being given to the parents of a teenage girl.

Between now and next time we meet, we would like each of you once to, do something different, when you catch Mary watching TV instead of doing what she needs to be doing, no matter how strange or weird or off-the-wall what you do might seem. The only important thing is that whatever you decide to do, you need to, do something different.

The "do something different" task is readily transferable to a wide variety of cases, in part because the wording is nonspecific. Since we do not prescribe a particular action, the clients can choose from a very wide range of possible ways to cooperate. Furthermore, the wording can be readily adapted by the therapist to fit the specifics of a case. Another distinct advantage is that therapists do not need to know specifically what it is the clients are already doing in order to use these formulas; that is, the complaint can be very vaguely constructed. This is fortunate since some clients find it very difficult to be specific in describing their own behavior in therapy sessions.

This skeleton key, "do something different," fits particular situations and yet is so generalized that it can be transferred from situation to situation without a lot of variation. Complaints seem to be structured very similarly across situations. A "spontaneous" small change in response to a generalized directive, "do something different," can prompt solutions. Quite frequently, the therapist cannot begin to predict what different response the clients will spontaneously develop.

Simply, solutions involve doing something different from what was done before that did not work. An example from outside the therapy situation illustrates this quite well.

COP BREATHES FEAR INTO BOY

Wichita, Kan. – AP – A 10-year-old boy told police he broke into a school to retrieve his homework so he could do it, but the confession came only after an officer threatened to hold his breath until the boy talked, police said.

Officers alerted to a prowler at a Wichita elementary school Sunday morning found the 10-year-old wandering around the building. The boy refused to talk, so officers took him in for questioning, according to a police report.

"When officers were unable to convince [him] to confess his intent, a mighty battle of wits began between the suspect and Lt. David Warry," the police report said.

The boy stood firm in the face of repeated questioning, saying little more than his name, according to the report.

"In exasperation, the lieutenant threatened to hold his breath until [the boy] confessed," the report said.

"This proved to be too much, and he blurted out that he had broken into the school to retrieve his homework so he wouldn't get a zero when school opened Monday" (*Milwaukee Journal*, 31 January 1984).

The particular complaint or type of complaint does not seem to matter much, and the particular different thing done does not seem to matter much either, as long as it is different enough and/or effective *and* it fits.

When clients describe what is troubling them, they usually describe all the "different" things they have found ineffective. However, a closer examination of these approaches frequently reveals that all of them are within the same logical class; they were, therefore, not different enough. Punishment is punishment, whether it be grounding, restricting, or yelling. Telling oneself to lose weight, dieting, having the doctor tell you to lose weight – all are the same class of behaviors if they do not produce the desired results. (Telling oneself or being told to start being a thin person might work.) Since clients seem not to find the different thing to do or the thing to do differently, they continue to complain.

How complaints develop in most cases is actually unknown. But we might (re)construct a history as if involving a whole tree of either/or decisions: (1) if the husband's coming home late is seen as normal the branch ends, if abnormal, the branch continues, and splits into (2) either he is bad or mad; (3) if bad, then a negative consequence is called for, if mad, treatment is called for. However, this is too simple because any split represents the frames of two people (husband and wife), and the fight is on over the interpretation given to the situation. When the decision "this is a bad husband and, therefore, he needs to be chastised" is called into question by the lack of results, then, rather than considering the behavior normal and ending their attempts to stop the lateness, they switch labels from bad to mad, and seek treatment, because they are still labeling it a "problem."

Frequently, the "do something different" task is most useful when clients complain about the ineffectiveness of their reaction to some repeating sequence of events, e.g., a child has temper tantrums to which the parents react in the same ineffective fashion. This direct but nonspecific intervention offers clients a wide range of possible new behaviors and insures that the chosen behavior will be something that fits for them and is not outside their bounds of possibility.

Case Example: Oreo Cookies

An eight-year-old boy was throwing temper tantrums both at home and in school. Typically he was given "time-outs" and lectures and sometimes spanked. But this approach did not stop the tantrums. Then both parents and school tried to reward him during the intervals between tantrums, but that did not work. The parents frequently found themselves yelling at the boy while the boy threw his tantrums. At the end of a session with just the parents, the therapist told them to, "Do something different next time Josh throws a tantrum, no matter how strange, or weird, or off-the-wall what you do might seem. The only important thing is that whatever you decide to do, you need to, do something different."

During the next tantrum father gave Josh a cookie without saying a single word. The tantrum stopped. When mother next witnessed a tantrum, she danced circles around the boy while he kicked and screamed. That tantrum stopped. Subsequently, neither the parents nor the school reported any tantrums. Both the cookie-giving and the dancing were behaviors previously excluded from the tantrum pattern, and their use proved different enough to prompt solution.

At first glance this solution appears to be counter-intuitive. Why should the cookie not serve as a reward or reinforcement rather than as a solution to the tantrum situation? It might seem as if father's behavior would promote tantrums rather than stop them, but it did not, because the tantrum-cookie sequence marked a new context in which the child did not know what to expect from father except that he knew he could not expect the usual attempts to stop the trantrum by punishments, lectures, or time-outs. It is possible that if the boy had thrown another tantrum and Dad gave him a cookie again rather than doing something else different, then the cookie might become a reinforcement. But, as it stands, the unique reaction proved a solution.

Case Example: Fear of the Unknown

Another couple, faced with similar tantrums and given the same task, reported that they had been unable to think of anything different to do. The need had never arisen, since their son had thrown no tantrums during the two-week interval. Unlike the first case, the boy had been present when the "do something different" task was assigned. The therapist then asked the boy about this lack of tantrums, and the boy replied, "I used to know exactly what they would do, but now I don't." He decided that rather than find out what different things his parents might do, he would just stop having tantrums. In this case, the parents did not have to think of something different to do because the boy found something different to do and the tantrums ceased completely.

Case Example: Bullshit*

After a year and a half of therapy that "was going nowhere," the parents brought their complaints about their 16-year-old son to new therapists. They complained about how "stupid" and "trite" Wayne's lies were; nonetheless, the parents still found them difficult to endure. They could not understand *why* Wayne needed to lie so much. They felt that they had tried everything: lectures, swatting, grounding, restricting him in other ways. But "nothing works with him."

After complimenting the parents on their persistence in this matter, the therapist commented that he was sure that the team had only seen the "tip of the iceberg." He suggested that they should not change anything yet, because things might get worse. The team also asked the family to observe, between sessions, what happened in their family that they wanted to continue to have happen. (See Chapter 9 for a detailed study of this "first session task".)

In the second session, the family talked for over a half hour about all the things they would like to continue to happen. When the therapist tried once again to set a concrete goal, the family found this impossible. They would "just know" because Wayne would be "feeling better about himself."

The team was struck by the family's sense of humor and told them that, as well as how impressed they were with the number of things they wanted to see continue. They continued with the following message:

> The team is split and confused by the difficulties you express and how best to correct them.
> (1) One team member says that there must be some deep underlying problem that is motivating this lying

---

*Steve Hunter and Arnold Woodruff, Youth Service Bureau, McHenry County, Illinois, reported on this therapy done by their team.

and stuff, and said something (vaguely) about some sort of complex that I don't understand. She feels that before we can figure this out, Wayne has to tell the most obvious and outrageous lie of his life with everyone in the family and every clue pointing at him. And that the absurdity of the situation will create the conditions under which everyone will understand "why" Wayne lies.

(2) A second team member feels that you are basically on the right track and should keep doing what you are doing in staying together as a team. In fact, this team member feels that Wayne's behavior may be keeping you together as a team. And that you should continue counseling and that, the next time Wayne lies, do something different, something that Wayne cannot expect.

(3) A third team member feels you are moving too far too fast with things and that you should go slow and be cautious about any further changes until you know "why" Wayne lies.

(4) I am thoroughly confused and exhausted by all this but think that all of you need to go home and think about, or get a clear sense of, when you'll know Wayne is better.

Three weeks later, the family reported that it had been a good interval, the one exception being the night Wayne came home three hours late and told the most outrageous lies. This convinced father that next time he needed to do something outrageously different. He decided to buy some cattle droppings from a neighbor and rub Wayne's face in the bullshit when next he was caught in a lie. Understandably, his wife would not let him do it, so he went to a novelty shop and bought a can labeled "bullshit repellent," which he had ready. The next time Wayne lied, father sprayed him with this. After the initial shock, everyone present saw the humor in the situation. Subsequently, during the rest of the interval (over two weeks) the parents did not catch Wayne in a single lie (a record period of time).

The therapist complimented Wayne on his performance of the "outrageous lie" task, father on his performance of the "outrageously different" task, and mother on two things, her good sense and her ability to stay out of these things between father and son (which was a different thing for her to do). The team warned the family about the process of change being three steps forward, two back, and suggested they watch out for the possibility of yet more outrageous lies. Father said he was ready.

The fourth session, which was held three weeks later, was opened with this question: "How many times did you need to repel Wayne's bullshit?" Father reported no need for the repellent and that he had found some "straightforward" ways to deal with Wayne the one or two times he thought he was lying. It turned out, however, that in both instances Wayne was being truthful.

After complimenting the family on the changes and worrying about future relapses, the team scheduled a "follow-up session" in two months, suggesting that the family might decide to cancel that if there was no need at that point.

Case Example: A Touch Is Worth Many Words

A mother complained about her 14-year-old deaf son's temper tantrums. When he was home from his residential school for only a weekend, things went fine. However, when he was home for an extended vacation, after a few days he would start to fight with Andy, his 11-year-old brother, refuse to do what he was told, make angry faces, slam doors, and run out of the house. This sort of behavior also occurred at school when he did not go home for a weekend. Once, immediately prior to the scheduling of the first session, mother and son's conflict had become physical.

During the first session it immediately became clear that all three cared deeply about one another. Although Jimmy said, "They talk funny," the mother's and Andy's signing was clear enough for Jimmy and the interpreter. Mother described her efforts to care for Jimmy and the difficult decision to place him in a residential school for his own best interest. He agreed that this school was better for him. Both of them described how pleasant things could be on the weekends, but expressed a lot of fear about the coming three-week holiday.

During the consulting break, the interpreter thought that Jimmy would have a difficult time understanding what we meant if we told him to "do something different." Remembering that mother had mentioned times when each surprised the other, the task was modified.

The therapist suggested that during the next week, if either of them thought things were getting close to another tantrum, then both of them should somehow pleasantly surprise the other. In fact, even when there were no "almost" tantrums, they were still to find a way to pleasantly surprise each other. Neither of them was to identify the surprise or ask, "Was that your surprise?" They were each to see if they could figure out how they were being surprised. The younger brother was given the job of observing this and reporting on how each of them surprised the other.

In the next session, Andy was able to tell us about the various surprises that he had observed. It had proved a hassle-free week, and the boys found ways to cooperate rather than fight. During this session it became clear that at least some of Jimmy's tantrums were part of a deliberate "game" of exaggeration. Sometimes mother's and Andy's misunderstanding of this ended in chaos. Neither his brother nor mother had been aware of this.

The therapist asked Jimmy to pretend to have a tantrum or to play this game at least once in the coming two-week period. Mother and brother were to guess when he was pretending and when he was serious. If they thought he was pretending, mother was to hug Jimmy, and Andy was to give him a brotherly squeeze on the arm. The idea behind this, which was not explained to them, was for mother and brother to communicate nonverbally with the deaf boy, which might be more real for him. This proved effective. In the next session, both mother and Andy reported following through, but since they had been unable to tell if the "tantrums" were real or pretend, they had physical contact "just in case." Jimmy said he was "pretending" all the time. In a subsequent phone conversation, mother reported that she could not tell real from pretend and had decided to treat all as pretend, "A hug is always the better thing." This seems to have eliminated the complaints both at home and at school.

Case Example: Anticipation

A young woman was very concerned about how depressed her husband was when he returned after a few days out of town. Each week he would spend two or three days out of town on business. When he walked in the front door of their house, he always seemed down-and-out. For the first couple of months, she tried cheering him up, but this did not work. He would just withdraw to his workshop. She tried talking with him about his feelings at various times, but he always said, "Nothing is wrong." She was afraid that he was not looking forward to coming home. She tried to make things especially cheerful, including having his best friends over when he returned or making his favorite meal. This did not work either and she became more worried. She asked her parents and her in-laws for advice, but they could not suggest anything except continuing to be cheerful in the face of his depression and her fears.

After hearing this description, the therapist told her to spend some time while her husband was gone figuring out what she thought her husband would be expecting her to do. Once she figured this out she was to "do something different." He told her that anything might make a difference and break this habit.

While her husband was out of town, she decided that what he would least be expecting was for her not to be home when he got there. She left a note on the kitchen door telling him that she would be home late. While he waited for her, he prepared his own dinner. He was not at all depressed when she arrived. The following week she was still painting the bathroom when he returned and he fixed dinner for both of them and gave no sign of feeling depressed. She decided that he had been feeling bad because she had been showing signs of missing him and so he felt guilty about having to be out of town so much. She decided that she would no longer let him know his being gone bothered her so much.

The "do something different" task seems to promote some random, or apparently random, behaviors in clients, allowing them to alter the sequences of behavior that are part of the complaints they brought to therapy. In part, this task seems to work because it reaffirms to the clients the therapist's expectation that change can and will happen, and that they, the clients, can change and solve the problem.

This task seems most useful when the complaint is an interactional one, i.e., when the parents are complaining about their child's behavior and/or their reactions to it, or one spouse is complaining about the behavior of the other and/or their reactions to it. The same idea, that it is necessary to "do something different," also applies when the person is complaining about his own behavior, but a different task seems more useful.

"PAY ATTENTION TO WHAT YOU DO WHEN YOU OVERCOME THE URGE TO . . . "

The main variation of the "do something different" task, "pay attention to what you do when you overcome the temptation or urge to . . . " (e.g., act depressed, overeat, yell at your spouse, get drunk), was designed for use when a person is complaining about his/her *own* behavior or about himself in some way.

Any complaint can be seen as if involving a rule, or a set of rules, which determines behavior. However, there are also exceptions to that rule. That is, although clients tend to say that the troublesome behavior *always* happens, there are some more or less similar conditions under which it does not happen. These exceptions can frequently serve as the best model upon which to build interventions because the behavior involved is already part of the clients' repertoire; consequently, the intervention will automatically fit. It will also be different because the exception is applied to the rule-bound situation, where it can serve as something new or random and thereby stand some chance of prompting new or different responses. Of course, pointing out this exception to clients may well not be very useful because of their "always" label on the behavior(s). They cannot see the exception as an exception; they see it as accidental and unrelated. It seems more useful for the therapist to help create a context in which clients can discover for themselves that some exceptions are possible and can be useful. The task, "pay attention to what you do when you overcome the temptation to . . . ," was designed specifically to help clients and therapist alike discover (and use) the exceptions to the rule.

Case Example: Flashback

A young woman came to therapy concerned that she might relapse into heavy drug use. Two years earlier she had successfully stopped using heroin and cocaine and even stopped smoking marijuana. Recently she had been more and more tempted to return to the old habits. As the urges increased she found herself cutting herself off from people and activities. At the first session she was asked to "pay attention to what you do when you overcome the urges to return to the old patterns involving drugs."

One week later she reported more activities, more social contacts, and no failures to overcome the urges. The task was repeated, and during the next session (two weeks after the second) she reported far fewer urges and more activities. Without the therapist's suggestion, she requested that the task be repeated, and the therapist gladly went along with the request. In the final session, two weeks later, she reported that the temptations had stopped and she was able to find time to relax and do nothing without the return of the urges.

The frame suggested by this task presupposes that the client (and clients in general) *will* overcome the urges or temptations (her frame suggested that the temptations would become too strong to resist) at least some of the time, and that the client will, perhaps, do something different in order to overcome the urges. The construction of the task is also meant to help the client pay attention to what she does, i.e., her behavior, rather than some interior state. In the session following the assignment of this task, the therapist frequently opens with a question such as, "Well, what did you do when you overcame the temptations during this past week?" This question presupposes that change has happened and that the client has done something to overcome at least some of the temptations. Regardless of the client's response, she is encouraged to see and use tools which she already has to overcome the temptation to "go back to the old way." Once the either/or thinking is reframed to include the excluded classes of behavior, the client will be able to do something different that fits for her, since it is her own, rather than the therapist's, idea.

Case Example: Who's First?

A mother and her 15-year-old son came to therapy because they both wanted to stop smoking. After exploring all the reasons for stopping or not stopping, the team gave the following variation of this homework task:*

> Between now and next session, pay attention to what you do when you overcome the temptation to smoke and pay attention to what the other one does when he or she overcomes the temptation to smoke. Half the team thinks that you, mother, will stop smoking

---

*This task, rather than the "do something different" task, was used because both mother and son were essentially making complaints about their own behavior, not about each other's smoking. If each had been complaining about the other, then the "do something different" task might have been more useful.

first, while the other half thinks that the son will stop
first. We don't know when you two will stop.

The message from the team presupposes that *both* mother
and son will stop smoking, the question now being who will
stop first and when. One week later, both mother and son
reported smoking far less and described in detail the various
alternate activities they found for themselves separately and
together. The team again wondered who would quit first.
Eventually (after a total of five sessions, all including this
same message from the team) both quit on the same day, each
claiming to have been first!
Eight months later neither was smoking.

Case Example: The Silent Critic

An older woman came to therapy because she wanted to
keep her job five more years until she retired. But at this
point she found herself becoming critical of her boss. Each
time this had happened in the past, she had spoken up and
lost her job. At her age she feared looking for another job.
She cared about this boss and was afraid that his careless
bookkeeping was going to lead to trouble. Every day the
pressure became worse as she found difficulty after difficulty.
The day before the first session, she felt so pressured by her
helpful urges that she had to quit early to prevent speaking
up.
The therapist, after complimenting her on withstanding
the pressure, asked her to count the number of urges she felt
each day and to pay attention to what she did to overcome
these urges. Each day she reported experiencing 15 to 20
urges. She overcame them all by shifting tasks, calling a
friend, chewing gum, watering plants, and once by correcting
the mistake without mentioning doing so, even though this
was not her job. Her boss noticed this correction and was
pleased with her initiative. But she was still afraid that he
would fire her if she pointed out mistakes or she corrected
them on her own.

After complimenting her on the ways she found to overcome the urges and on taking the initiative, the therapist remarked that her boss was lucky to have someone so sensitive working for him and wondered if he knew how lucky he was. He gave her the same task.

Again she found things to do instead of being critical. This turned out to be a good thing for her when her boss complimented her on "not mothering" him. This reinforced her decision not to become critical. However, she felt the pressure increased. To overcome the temptations, she took on more and more responsibility for various tasks around the office, including correcting errors without being told.

Six months later, he gave her a substantial raise because she was so conscientious about her work and able to work without a lot of directives.

CONCLUSION

The formula interventions and the case material illustrate the creativity of clients and the resources they already have before they come to therapy. In some sense, the therapy really adds nothing (the Wizard of Oz technique): The therapist does not tell the clients what to do differently and does not teach the clients any new techniques. These interventions are minimally intrusive and yet their impact seems inordinately large. The ripple effect or the concept of wholism gives us some notions about how a small difference can become a big enough difference.

9

CHANGE IS NOT ONLY POSSIBLE, BUT INEVITABLE

FIRST SESSION FORMULA TASK

"Between now and next time we meet, we [I] would like you to observe, so that you can describe to us [me] next time, what happens in your [pick one: family, life, marriage, relationship] that you want to continue to have happen" (de Shazer, 1984; de Shazer and Molnar, 1984b).

The continued use of the crystal ball technique (Chapter 5) and the formula tasks (Chapter 8) led to this formula intervention, which was developed in mid-1982 by de Shazer and Nunnally. The first session task was designed to shift the clients' focus from the past to present and future events and implicitly to promote expectations of change. Clients frequently expect things to go poorly and this message strongly suggests that the therapist and the team have different expectations: Something worth continuing to have happen is going to happen; in fact, worthwhile things are already happening – watch for them. The message leaves no doubt about this. The phrasing does not include even an implicit "if." While the therapists' expectations are considerably different from the clients' expectations, the task continues to enable the therapists to fit with the clients' goals and their vagueness. The results of the crystal ball technique suggest it is this difference in expectations that seems to make a difference in the clients' responses in the following session.

Like the other formula tasks, this one was first designed and used with a specific case. The concrete and behavioral focus of the response startled the team. A family that appeared rather hopeless and described their situation in very vague terms turned itself around between the first and second sessions. Not only had worthwhile things been observed, but some of these worthwhile happenings were *new* behaviors and in the area of the complaint. This prompted us to start using the formula intervention with other cases in which the clients described vague goals and complaints. Case after case, concrete and specific changes in the week interval between the first and second session were reoported. This prompted the development of a more organized study, which is described later in this chapter.

Because of the formula's wording and the built-in expectation of at least a change in perception, many clients easily find a way to cooperate with this task. Of course, not all clients respond to this task with solutions, but most do describe some specific worthwhile happenings. Some of the events reported are continuations of things that were happening before therapy started, but many describe what happened as "new" or "different." This alone would be enough to justify continued use of the task. Unlike the "structured fight" task and the "do something different" tasks described in Chapter 8, the first session task is not tied to prompting solutions in situations where clients describe a particular sort of troublesome pattern.

This task *fits* the framing frequently described by clients — *things happen*, which implies, of course, that the clients do not have control over what happens. The clients see themselves simply as victims. Traditionally, this sort of definition was used for "symptoms," things that "happen" to clients which are negative. The task can be seen as an attempt to promote the substitution of a more beneficial symptom, one that the client wants to continue to have happen. This notion is derived from Erickson's "Special Techniques of Brief Hyp-

notherapy" (1951a; in Haley, 1967b, pp. 390–409), in which
Erickson describes his unique version of "symptom substitution" to solve problems.

Furthermore, the task is designed to create a self-fulfilling
prophecy about the future course of events. There is an attempt to promote the Rosenthal effect (1966), where the bias
of the teacher affected the test scores of their students. If the
teacher expected the student to suddenly blossom, there was
a likelihood that the student would blossom. Here the prophecy is that something worthwhile is going to be *noticed* between the first and second sessions, and the likelihood is that,
indeed, that will be the case.

Case Example: Three Guns

A family came to therapy in a panic. The parents had
found that one of their pistols was missing from their room.
After searching around, they found the loaded gun wrapped
in a ski mask in their 19-year-old son's room. They did not
know what to make of this. When confronted, Mickey said
he was going to use it for target practice on the back 40.
However, the ski mask suggested something else. Mother
wondered if the loaded gun was meant to be used for suicide
or for the murder of both parents, while Dad wondered if the
boy was planning a heist.

The day before this episode, Mickey had registered for the
coming semester in college and had paid his fees. However,
after this episode, he was talking about going to Canada instead of returning to school. The parents did not like this
idea, but they also did not like the idea of worrying about
what the loaded gun might mean. Mickey's going to Canada
would be better than continuing this crisis situation, but
what they really wanted was for Mickey to go to school (and
like it) and to solve whatever the trouble was. In fact, mother
had given the boy an ultimatum: either go to school and
get therapy or leave by dinnertime that day. If he refused to
leave or go to school, *she* would leave. However, none of the
three could agree about what good anybody's leaving might

do. But *something* had to be done! Naturally, none of them was able to describe a concrete and specific goal for therapy that all could agree upon: Father wanted the boy back in school, mother wanted to understand the "problem," while Mickey saw nothing that could not be solved by leaving home.

After the consulting break, the therapist gave them a series of compliments based on their willingness to sacrifice to solve the problem and on the support each was giving to the other. He also suggested that any decisions be put on hold, since a crisis usually led to bad decisions. All three agreed. Then the therapist gave them the first session task and told father to remove all the guns from the house.

One week later a changed family appeared. During the interval (1) Mickey had decided to go back to college, but (2) to live in a dorm rather than at home. (3) Instead of getting mother to set this up for him, he did it himself, which mother saw as a sign of maturity. (4) He had volunteered to help Dad with some painting around the house. (5) Mickey had also talked with his parents about some of his troubles, although not about the "why" behind the loaded gun. (6) On two days mother had gone out of her way to make and pack a lunch for Mickey. (7) Mickey had, without being asked, taken care of mother's dogs when she was delayed getting home.

These seven events were reported by the family as things that happened which they wanted to have continue to have happen. Several (3, 4, 5, and 7) were described as "new or different." In fact, all three described the interval as a "better week." The intervention message (in this second session) focused on the changes the family had made and cautioned them about the probability of a setback. During the third session, which turned out to be the last, the family again reported more things they wanted to have continue to have happen, all of which were continuations of the same new classes of behavior. The team again worried about a relapse. Follow-up indicated that the new patterns continued and Mickey returned to school.

Case Example: Just Sixteen

Sue, 16, her mother, and her grandparents, with whom she lived, came to therapy after the girl had been returned from an extended runaway. Sue's mother believed Sue would never change, since she had always been a problem. The grandmother saw Sue as basically a good kid "when she wanted to be" and saw herself as "too soft"; she had difficulty following through on consequences. Grandfather saw his being too busy with the many farming tasks as contributing to the difficulties. Everyone agreed, however, that when he did say "no" he meant it and people listened. Sue essentially agreed with her grandmother and defended herself against her mother.

Goals were established during the first session. These included Sue's doing the assigned household chores, talking more with her grandparents, coming home on time (once the grounding was lifted), and informing them of any changes in agreed upon plans. After the consulting break, the family received the following feedback from the team:

> Mother received her feedback first. The team was impressed that she was still working to resolve the complicated problem even though she felt like giving up. The team was particularly impressed that she was such a good mother since they appreciated how difficult it must have been for her to decide to part with her daughter even though it was for her daughter's well-being. Some mothers might selfishly insist that their daughters remain with them regardless of the environment. The team added a metaphor directed at both mother-daughter sets about how connected mothers and daughters are and how difficult it sometimes is to separate. The team also appreciated her pessimism about Sue because, after having been hurt so much by Sue, there would be a danger in being optimistic too soon.
>
> Grandmother was told that the team was impressed that she was able to see positive things in Sue even

though her behavior was unacceptable at this time. The team noticed how sensitive and caring grandmother was for Sue's feelings. She demonstrated this by wanting not only that Sue do her chores at home, but that she not be dissatisfied nor unhappy about it. Many grandparents would be satisfied with having the task done. Finally, the team was struck by her knowledge that being a "softie" may be part of the problem – many people never see the connection.

Grandfather was complimented on his ability to set limits and on his intention to do so in the future.

Sue was complimented on her accepting some responsibility for the problem and (since she said little during the session) for knowing when to remain quiet (Weiner-Davis, 1984).

The formula first session task was then given as "homework." In the following session, the grandparents reported that things were much better throughout the two weeks. Sue did misbehave, but grandmother stuck to her guns; when she felt like giving in, she turned to grandfather for support. Sue had been doing her chores and talking more around the house. After complimenting them all on the changes they had made, the team worried about a relapse since "real change is three steps forward and two back."

In the third and final session, the reports continued on the same track. In fact, even school performance had improved. Surprisingly, Sue had stayed home one weekend evening with her grandparents. Sue and her mother had been going out once each week together and were enjoying this. Once again, the team expressed some concern about a relapse and the grandparents promised to be in touch should there ever be any "big problems" in the future.

Case Example: Trying Once Again

After years of therapy with various therapists during their 13 years of marriage, a couple came to BFTC. At times the

wife had found the therapy useful, but in general the husband
had always been dissatisfied and had, therefore, dropped out.
Both seemed bitter and hostile towards each other and described their married life as stressful and conflictual. They
had large, global goals which they had had for years, but
therapy had not helped them reach these goals. Some minimal goal needed to be established, so that both could know
this therapy worked. They agreed with this idea and suggested that they would know progress had been made when
they were able to share a laugh now and then.

Frequently during the initial interview with a couple it is
necessary to establish further what they want out of therapy.
One of the techniques we have developed involves simple scaling questions. "On a scale from 1 to 10, with 10 being the
highest level possible for you right now, how much do you
want this marriage?" The husband responded with a 10 and
the wife with a 9. Clearly, both wanted the marriage to continue. It is also important then to investigate this further,
because one or the other might perceive the other as unwilling
to do anything to *make* these wishes come true. "On the same
sort of scale, what do you think the chances are that this marriage will survive?" The husband responded with an 8, the
wife a 6. These relatively high numbers surprised both the
therapist in the room and the rest of the team behind the mirror. The couple's motivation affected the design of the intervention message:

> First of all, we're impressed with the persistence
> you both have shown by hanging in there, trying
> to . . . solve the problem. Many couples, describing
> what you've described, would have given up long ago.
> We hope that you will let us know if we are not the
> right kind of help for you.
>
> We were also struck by the fact that you both gave
> higher numbers to the level of wanting this marriage
> and the chances of making it together, higher than
> any of the team had anticipated. Clearly, this indi-
> cates to us that you must know something about

your relationship that we don't know, yet and, therefore, between now and next time we meet, we want
you to observe, so you can tell us about it, what happens in your relationship that you want to continue
to have happen.

Two weeks later, both reported that things between them
were "better." He was pleased with the good experiences he
had had putting the two children, aged four and six, to bed
on several nights, and she was pleased with the way in which
he had welcomed her mother when she arrived for an extended
visit. What they both described as "better" was that they
became aware that things were not always "down," but that
things were both "up and down" throughout the two weeks.
As much as possible, the therapist focused the remainder of
the session on the "up" parts of the weeks. At the end of the
session, he gave them the following message:

At this point, we have a better picture of how come
your desire to stay together is so high – which puzzled
us last time. Yet it is still not a clear picture to us,
so making specific suggestions is difficult. As a whole,
the team is guessing that you shouldn't change things,
yet, because a wrong change could make things worse.
But I think taking a brisk, half-hour walk every other
day couldn't hurt.

The therapeutic problem had been constructed as the couple's need to clear up for the team the reasons they wanted
to stay together. This, of course, meant that the couple had
to do something different to prove and justify the high numbers. They had to change in order to live up to their own levels
of both desire and conviction. This made it easier for the
therapist to focus on change rather than on complaints (thus
promoting further change). It also made it easier for the team
to compliment the couple on their changes in the following
session.

At that session they reported that they had decided that

walking together was a good idea since it gave them time away from the children. She had called him at work, which she had not done in years, and had found someone to clean house and care for the children on alternate Saturdays so they would have more time together. At the end of the session, they were given this message:

> We're pleased that things are really moving in the right direction and that you both know there are potholes on any road to wherever you want to go. Now, we are becoming afraid that you two are traveling too fast on this uncharted road and we're afraid that you'll become overconfident and, if by chance you hit a pothole, it'll feel like a pit dug into the road. And, we are afraid you're risk-takers and, therefore, suggest you keep things going in the same direction but slowly, avoiding dangerous curves, strange routes, and detours.

One month later they reported having had some laughs together and being nice to each other for most of the whole month. However, they did not feel confident about their being able to keep it up, and therefore a follow-up session was scheduled in another month. The team, under these conditions, openly worried about relapsing or falling into pits on the road. The follow-up session included news that they had gone out of town for a couple of days without the children, which they had never done before. They were talking and laughing more together.

Case Example: Is Persistence a Virtue?

In their thirtieth year of marriage, a couple came to therapy. Each complained about the other's present and past. Throughout the years they had never seen "eye to eye" about anything. They described a bleak picture of life together, even while they had raised four children quite successfully. When one complained about anything, the other matched it. Complaint was traded for complaint; neither defended. The main point they agreed on was that they wanted a better marriage as a result of coming to therapy. They also agreed that it was necessary for the other person to change in order to reach that goal. The therapist used the scaling questions to help get a better picture of what the couple wanted. On the scale from 1 to 10, each responded with a 4 in regards to how much he or she wanted the marriage, and the husband guessed a 3 while the wife placed herself at 4 on how good the chances were that the marriage would survive.

In effect, they were both saying that they did not want the marriage more than they wanted it, and they gave the marriage far less than a 50-50 chance. Yet they *said* they wanted a better marriage as a result of therapy.

The team complimented them on hanging in there in spite of the bad luck they had experienced and suggested that many couples faced with the same situations year after year would not have stayed together for 30 years. Therefore, the team was puzzled by what held the marriage together and hoped that they could give us more information about that during the next session. The therapist then assigned the first session task.

During the second session, the wife reported being pleased with the way the two of them went about deciding what to do on Sunday afternoon, but the husband saw the same event as just another example of her wrongheadedness. She then withdrew the claim that the decision-making was something worth having happen again and said "nothing" worthwhile had happened. He fully agreed, jokingly suggesting, however, that he had used a magnifying glass all week looking for something worthwhile. Aside from having stayed together for the kids and for their own parents, they had no ideas about why this marriage had lasted 30 years.

The team suggested that, since things were so bad, it would be foolhardy to rush into changing anything because the odds were that a "wrong change" would only make things worse. Particularly since they did not see "eye to eye" about anything, any change could be a wrong change which would make things worse. On the one hand, a divorce might result; on the other hand, one or the other might feel worse about the status quo. At least they were used to the way things were. The team members said that they did not want to risk even an accidental change; therefore, they suggested that the couple go home and think about if they were willing to take the risk of a divorce or of changing things, which might make things even worse. The next appointment was set for four weeks later, so that the team would not accidentally pressure them into a decision.

Since things were so bad between these spouses and yet they *said* they wanted a better marriage, the team decided on a cautious approach. They were serious in suggesting that the couple not change anything without considering the consequences. The couple had attempted to perform the first task in a straightforward manner; the team, therefore, expected them to do the same with this "change nothing" task.

One month later the spouses returned, each having separately decided one week earlier that a divorce was the thing to do. Since they had told one another about the decision, things were more relaxed between them. They had made plans to jointly file the necessary papers.

The team agreed with them that living apart probably could not be any worse than continuing to live together while hating being together. In fact, the team agreed that things might be better for both of them. The only question the team had was: Which one will living separately be better for the soonest? The partners were asked to keep track of how soon after they began living separately they began to feel better and, at that time, to send a postcard. (Follow-up through the referral source indicates that after six months of living separately both are doing better. Since no postcards have arrived, it may not be "better enough" – yet.)

A STUDY

The concreteness of the family's responses to this intervention in the first case example led BFTC's therapists to use the same task in other more or less vague situations (complaint and/or goals undefined). The results of repeated use indicated that clients tended to respond to this message in rather concrete and specific terms. Therefore, de Shazer and Molnar designed an exploratory study to find out:

(a) if the pattern of concrete responses held over a larger number of cases;

(b) what criteria were used for deciding when to use the first session task and when not to use it;

(c) if "new and/or different" behavior occurred with any regularity between session one and session two (usually a one-week interval);

(d) if creating clients' expectation of worthwhile events did lead to the reporting of worthwhile events and behaviors;

(e) if these reported worthwhile things would have some perceived durability;

(f) if this approach would lower our average number of sessions per client; and

(g) if this approach would prove somewhat more successful (in terms of "success" reported at follow-up) than our usual results in cases where the task had not been used.

During the study, the therapists used the formula first session task except when there were clear reasons against it. In part, our reasoning in making this task "first choice" was that when the therapist and team were able to identify specific areas and goals for therapy, then a concrete and specific task was indicated; this was not problematic for BFTC's therapists. However, more often than not clients came to therapy with general distress and vague complaints. Furthermore, this approach would result in a larger sample than would instruction to "use the first session task when you want to."

As part of the study, the therapists were asked to open the second session by asking: "What happened since last time we met that you want to continue to have happen?" Then, after the session, the therapists and/or the team member(s) behind the mirror were asked to fill out a simple one-page form (see Figure 9.1).

Using this report form has led to a greater understanding of the elements a therapist needs to consider in building interventions. It is clear that a pattern of therapist-client interaction develops from session to session and the information about the clients and their complaints becomes clarified and more specific. This has led to a rather complex decision tree, which therapists can use to guide them in achieving fit. For the sake of clarity, this tree will be described branch by branch, considering each factor in turn, even though the branches interconnect and interact. Before designing an intervention message in a second or later session, the therapist needs to study the client's responses to the previous session.

Better, Same, or Worse?

Does the clients' report indicate that things are: (a) better, (b) the same, or (c) worse? (See Figure 9.2.) Most often the answer is only implied by the quantity and quality of their reports on what worthwhile things they observed. Asking the question directly can be useful, since some clients report that many worthwhile things happened and yet nothing at all is better in the area of the complaint. This seemingly incongruous report might indicate that they view the complaint as separate and not connected to the rest of their lives — particularly to anything worthwhile.

This general sense of how things are going is important for many reasons. It helps to inform the therapist about the degree of fit achieved in the previous session(s) and shows how the cooperating relationship is developing. If things are *better*, the clients' expectations for continued improvement are developing and, therefore, the therapist needs to keep in mind the probable usefulness of a "relapse" warning when he designs his interventions. If things are *the same*, the therapist might consider this a sign that the clients are doing something that is good for them, since things are not worse. Since clients probably expect things to go from bad to worse,

Figure 9.1   Research Report Form – 1982, Project #1

Family Name _____
Therapist _____
Dates: Session #1 _____   Session #2 _____

Invariant First Session Task

"Between now and next time we meet, we (I) would like you
to observe, so that you can describe to us (me) next time, what
happens in your (family, marriage, relationship, life) that you
want to continue to have happen."

(Therapist describe: If you do not use this, how did you (team) decide
it would be better not to do this? Be concise. Use reverse side if necessary.)

*   *   *

Session Two

Question to client: "What happened that you want to continue to have
happen?"

Check: _____ Nothing   _____ Something
Check: _____ Vague   _____ Concrete

If concrete, list specifics:

*   *   *

Did the *clients* define their behavior between session 1 and session
2 as "different than before the first session"?

Check: _____ Yes   _____ No

Did the clients report that the situation that brought them in is:

Check: _____ Worse   _____ Same   _____ Better

Figure 9.2

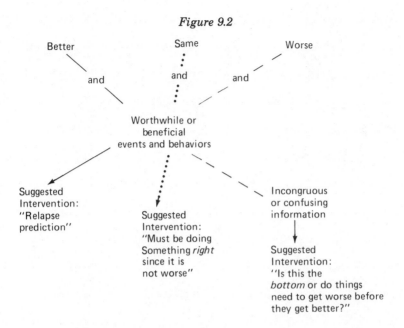

this can be a useful reframing. If things are *worse*, it is sometimes useful for the therapist to keep in mind when designing an intervention message that sometimes things have to get worse before they get better; therefore, he might wonder with the clients if this is really the bottom or if things need to go from worse to worst before they can get better.

Worthwhile and/or Beneficial Events and Behaviors?

The responses to the first session task proved to us how important it is for the therapist to find out what things the clients did and/or observed between sessions. (See Figure 9.3.) Since observed change can happen quickly, what the clients are doing that is good for them can, of course, be used to further promote solutions even though the particular examples are outside the complaint area. Furthermore, clients' ways of reacting to worthwhile events can be used as models for de-

Figure 9.3

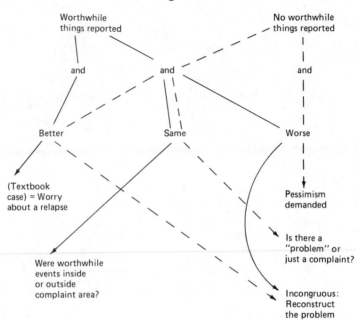

veloping solution-promoting behaviors and frames. Although new and/or different behaviors are often seen as the best indication of changes or of movement toward solution, old behaviors that the clients are learning to use in different situations can be equally revealing. In fact, since transferred behaviors automatically fit, they can be more useful in some situations.

Since most clients given the first session task report their observations in concrete terms, it can be useful for the therapist to think about using specific and concrete tasks as part of his therapeutic reaction. A small minority of clients will only be able to describe these worthwhile events in vague and/or confusing terms. When this happens, the therapist needs to construct his message in vague terms as well and to openly express his own confusion. If things are reported as "somehow better," the therapist might vaguely talk about the probability that things will get worse again. Keeping in mind the idea of tit for tat, the therapist reacts in a way that is vague and confusing but still somehow different. At this point, this kind of reaction is more likely to promote cooperation and to achieve a fit than any concrete, specific intervention.

If clients report that *nothing* worthwhile has happened, the therapist should find out if they misunderstood the task and are saying "no" to worthwhile things *just in the area of the complaint.* Once that is clarified, clients seldom persist throughout the whole of the second session with a negative report, but now and then it does happen. Of course, this is a depressing state of affairs and the therapist needs to recognize it as such. A message with some pessimism about the speed of expected change is useful here.

More often clients reporting initially that nothing worthwhile happened will, nonetheless, report that things are somehow better, even though they are unable to see "why" things are better. It is often useful in this situation to compliment the clients on obviously having done something right since normally things have to get worse before they get better. It is sometimes useful to then give them the task of watching what they do right so that things do not get any worse.

Inside and/or Outside the Complaint Area?

It is our experience that clients' reports of worthwhile things can include behaviors and events inside the complaint area, outside the complaint area, and both inside and outside (see Figure 9.4). But even when the things that the clients want to see continue are clearly outside the complaint area, some clients will report less concern with the complaint itself. This difference in their situation can lead to further success and should not be minimized. In fact, the complaint may continue to decrease in importance over the next interval between sessions. But this can only happen if the other things either continue to improve or, at the least, do not get worse. Therefore, these changes outside the complaint area need to

Figure 9.4

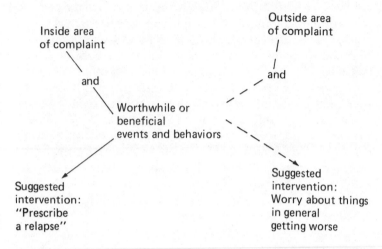

be seen by the therapist as part of the milieu of the complaint and treated accordingly. Since any event that makes things more satisfactory can potentially be part of the solution, it is again legitimate to worry about a relapse of some sort.

Results

Reporting the results of the first session task has been routine since the start of the project. The following figures are from two different months, six months apart. This is an exploratory, clinical study designed to check on our clinical impression that clients given the first sesion task

   (a) frequently reported the observation of worthwhile hap-
       penings,
   (b) frequently reached their goals in fewer sessions, and
   (c) were less likely to fail to reach their goals.

This study is not to be mistaken for formal research. We only set out to explore the process of change, not to confirm a theory or hypothesis.

(1) The task was given to 56 (64%) of the 88 new clients seen. Of these 50 (89%) reported that something worthwhile had happened, while 6 (11%) did not report anything happening that they wanted to continue to have happen. All of the 50 gave their reports in terms the therapists considered to be concrete and specific.
(2) 46 (82%) reported that at least one of the events they wanted to continue to have happen was new or different.
(3) 32 (57%) reported that things were "better," while 19 (34%) reported things were "the same." Only 5 (9%) reported things as "worse."
(4) Of the 24 reporting "same or worse," 19 (79%) gave incongruous reports such as, "Yes, something worthwhile had happened, but things are either the same or worse" (de Shazer and Molnar, 1984b).

Follow-up

In spite of great persistence*, we were able to contact for follow-up only 28 of the 56 who were given the first session task. In each case, therapy had been finished for at least six months but no more than one year. The follow-up questionnaire is shown in Figure 9.5. With the exception of the third question, which is focused on the reports of change given in response to the first session task, the questions are the same as those used at the Brief Therapy Center of the Mental Research Institute (Fisch, 1983), and again, with the exception of the third, are used for our routine follow-up. This gives us a standard for comparison, although not a real control group, except that many of the same therapists were involved in both the routine and the special studies. It is important to remember that this is not "formal research"; rather, it is a clinical and theoretical study. In a sense, it is experimental philosophy. As a team, we have philosophical concepts about

*Maureen McCarty and Carol Michalski, both graduate students at BFTC, did the follow-up phone calls. A special thanks to them for their persistence.

Figure 9.5 Follow-up Questionnaire, 1983–4

1. "When you came to therapy, your main complaint was . . . " (be specific about this). "Is this better?" (If "yes," go to #2.) If "no," then ask, "Is this the same?" (If "same," go to #2.) If not, then ask, "Is it worse?" before going to 2.
1a. Better   1b. Same   1c. Worse

2. "You were also concerned about . . . " (be specific). "Is this better, same, worse?" (If there was a secondary or related complaint. If not, go to #3.)
2a. Better   2b. Same   2c. Worse

3. "During therapy, you noticed a change in . . . " (be specific). "Is this continuing?"
3a. Yes   3b. No

4. "Have any new problems arisen since you finished therapy at BFTC?"
4a. Yes   4b. No

5. "Have any old problems that were not directly dealt with in therapy improved since you finished therapy at BFTC?"
5a. Yes   5b. No

6. "Has any member of the family (if a family unit was seen), or have you or your spouse, or have you seen another therapist or counselor since you finished at BFTC about . . . " (be specific, again listing the original complaint).
6a. Yes   6b. No

the nature of therapeutic change and this entire project is designed as a test: Are we going in the right direction?

Indeed, the responses indicate that we are headed in the right direction.

(1) 23 of the 28 (82%) given the task report that things are better. It must be noted that the "better responses to questions 1 and 2 do not necessarily mean a "cure"; rather, they indicate that the things they complained about at the start of therapy are "better enough that they are not now in therapy."

(2) Of particular importance to this study is that after a minimum of 6 months, some (at least one) of the specifically named worthwhile things reported in the second session are continuing to happen in 21 of 23 successful cases and in 2 of the 5 failures. This is not just a simple matter of satisfaction. The clients reported that specific new behaviors or types of events were continuing to happen. This at least suggests that essentially spontaneous changes, seen perhaps as a result of the task, have some permanence. The reports given in the second session are not just flashes in the pan; changes noted during the first weeks of therapy seem to make the therapy more effective.

At the start of the project, we made two other predictions: (a) more clients would report that things were better in the area of the main complaint than our usual follow-up indicated, and (b) the average number of sessions would be lower than our average of six.

(3) Of those we were able to contact, 23 of 28 (82%) reported that their main complaint is "better." This compares favorably with our typical follow-up figure of 72%.

(4) 25 of the 28 had mentioned a secondary complaint during therapy (although it was not necessarily dealt with) and 11 of them (all from the successes) indicated that things are better in this area too.

(5) Another instance of the ripple effect is also reported by 15 of the successes who reported other improvements in areas not dealt with in therapy.

(6) In past follow-up studies, 6 was the average number of sessions, but in this one the average number of sessions was only 5.

(7) 16 of the successes reported that no new complaints had developed since the end of therapy, while 8 reported that some new troubles had developed but they were not bad enough to require therapy.

Discussion

It seems that the occurrence of changes early in therapy
is related to both the number of sessions and the outcome of
the therapy in terms of the complaint. Since changes are
observed and reported by the second session, the expectation
of significant change in the area of the complaint, as well as
of a solution, is reaffirmed for both therapist and client. Thus,
cooperation between the client and therapist is promoted.
Cooperating is also promoted by the idea that there is a
future solution. This future is more salient to the client because there has already been evidence of a significant difference.

Prior to the start of the project, de Shazer and Molnar had
heard from colleagues about several uses of the first session
task and the responses clients gave in the second session.
This led us to assume that the clients' reports of "something
worth continuing to have happen" and/or "new or different
happenings" would change the therapists' way of handling the
second session. We assumed that therapists would respond
to these positive reports with an *open* expectation of *continuing* change. The frequency with which clients reported
new and different behavior in the complaint pattern itself offered some confirmation of the notion that change is con-
tinuous or at least that significant changes can be made
quickly, a view strengthened by the follow-up phase of the
project. Indeed, this is what happened. Therapists started to
see change in the second session and, therefore, found themselves with success on their hands. Then they had to worry
out loud about the possibility of a relapse or face disappointed
clients in the third session. Another change quickly followed.
Thereafter therapists started the second and following sessions with the same question about what had happened that
the clients wanted to continue to have happen or an alternative about what the client was doing that was good for him.

The whole team was surprised by yet another finding: the
concrete and specific nature of the clients' response reports.
Brief therapists (de Shazer, 1975a, 1982a; Fisch et al., 1983;

Haley, 1963; Watzlawick et al., 1974; Weakland et al., 1974) like goals expressed in concrete, specific terms because measurement of failure and success is easier. This leads them to want concrete and specific complaints, as well as concrete and specific changes. However, not all clients (even with the aid of concrete-minded therapists) are able to define their concerns and their goals this way.

Since clients report concrete behavioral changes in response to the task, the continuation of the changes already initiated can be used by the therapist as a goal. When these first changes are described as happening within the problematic pattern, then the goal of brief therapy can be seen as met: Change has been initiated and solution is underway. All the therapist then needs to do is work with the clients on keeping things the same! Or, to slip into another framework, the therapist can help the clients reinforce the desired changes. Ericksonian techniques, such as worrying about, predicting, prescribing, or even demanding a relapse, have been developed for just this situation. The task of therapy shifts from initiating change to preventing a relapse and/or promoting the ripple effect. The follow-up seems to indicate that the therapists were rather successful in this.

The study changed the behavior of the therapists in a number of ways. Most importantly, the project promoted the therapists' expression of their expectation of change and their expectation of rapid change. This shift in gears prompts further expectations of change. Since change might be in desirable or undesirable directions, the therapist must pay attention to potential relapses, as well as potential ripples.

Although the numbers are too small, the follow-up phase of the study also seems to confirm the success of the first session task as a therapeutic tool that helps to promote change and solution. Most of the clients given this task (whom we were able to contact) report both that the area of complaint continues to be better and that the worthwhile happenings are continuing to happen six months to a year after therapy.

10

CONCLUSIONS

RULES OF THUMB

Over the years of watching therapists work effectively and of watching the videotapes of my own work, I have noticed that there are certain heuristics or unwritten guidelines that are frequently used when constructing problems and, therefore, solutions. Some of these have been explicitly or implicitly described in the previous chapters; they are collected here for pragmatic reasons. These more or less simple guides can be useful in helping the therapist focus on aspects of the situation which can readily be utilized for designing the problem and for achieving fit. Of course, these hints may not prove useful in any particular case and none of them is *always* useful, but in any particular situation exploring these may prove useful in focusing on a potential solution.

Past Successes

With great frequency a client will describe the complaint in universal terms, bemoaning his helplessness in the face of the unsolvable. Sometimes, as the interview evolves, he or she will point out some past success. He may see this as un-related, although the therapist believes it to be exactly what the client needs to do to solve the problem. The client's reality and the therapist's reality are too different for this to be useful news. It does no good to point this out. Rather, it is the kind of thing the therapist needs to know and to remember for future use.

Furthermore, it does not seem at all useful for the therapist to explore how the past success in situation A is different from the current complaint situation B. The difference is a given. What the therapist needs to do in his efforts at problem construction is to create a link between situation A and situation B. Any similarities might be usefully noted, but again this is something for the therapist to know. Even this similarity might be too different for the client. Making an indirect link between A and B is more useful than attempting to formulate, with the client, a version of reality in which A and B are similar.

For instance, a young lady complained about her "low self-esteem," which was evidenced by her inability to make decisions. In fact, she found that even when she did make a decision, she usually would not be able to stick to it if anyone was in the least critical. This criticism did not need to be spoken; it could be implied or she could even read it into a situation. As the interview progressed, she told about her boyfriend's drinking and how that made it difficult for her to stay away from drinking. She had, on her own, stopped drinking two years previously.

Here was a decision which she had made and stuck to in spite of grave temptations, since her resumption of drinking would have stopped their arguments.

The therapist complimented her on having stopped drinking and on having stuck to this decision when many other people, maybe even most, would have been unable to stick to it. She was further complimented on not forcing herself into making decisions which she thought, perhaps unconsciously, might not be so good for her. Therefore, she should continue to wonder about any and every possible decision. She followed this advice for several weeks before making two decisions which were good for her.

Exceptions to the Rule

In many ways, exceptions to the rule are very similar to past successes, except that exceptions are clearly within the realm of the complaint. Simply, nothing *always* happens;

nothing is *always* the same. But, since the client punctuates the complaint as "always," the exceptions are seen as events totally outside the complaint rather than as potential solutions. The therapist needs to note any and all exceptions which can be useful for constructing tasks.

For instance, a couple complained about their getting into verbal fights every Thursday night when he returned from bowling at 11:30. Week after week they found something to argue about, but neither could remember any of the details. On Friday they were still angry until his parents came over for their weekly dinner visit. Then they were able to be nice to each other; this would continue until Thursday. Having been in therapy before, she voluntarily denied bad feelings about his bowling and also quickly denied having bad feelings towards his parents who had done so much for them. A complete mystery.

As they detailed the history of these fights, he remembered once when she had been next door visiting when he got home, and so he gratefully went to bed before her return. She came home a half hour later expecting a fight and was surprised to find him asleep. That week there was no fight.

The therapist noted this exception and a homework task was devised based on it. She was asked to experimentally toss a coin on the following two Thursdays at 10:30. Heads, she was to leave the house until after his return; tails, she was to behave normally. He was to write down, in detail, his thoughts on the way home on each Thursday; then, both were to notice any difference. This task construction had the potential of making a difference even if the coin should come up tails, since he might be coming home with the expectation that she would not be there. Furthermore, behaving normally because you are told to is different from normal behavior.

She was home on both Thursdays but they did not have a fight on either. As he said, he did not know what to expect so he did not think about the crap on the way home that he usually thought about. She did not toss the coin at all, but rather had a pleasant surprise ready each time—freshly baked cookies. Fights on Thursday night ceased to be a matter of complaint.

The "Either/Or" Rule

Sometimes clients' complaints can be clearly seen as set in a context, explicit or implicit, that says, "I am right; you are wrong." Spouses who each hold this point of view can find living together extremely frustrating, since they do not even have the illusion of possible compromise. Therefore, when they come for therapy, each one wants the therapist to join in declaring the other "wrong." However, it is not useful for the therapist to declare one, or the other, or even both, "wrong."

Shortly after their wedding a husband began complaining about his wife's desire to continue her "night out with the girls" once a week. He thought that people in love would not want to do that; rather, they would want to spend every possible moment together. Therefore, he reluctantly came to the conclusion that she did not really love him (the "out of sight, out of mind" position).

The wife saw his position as "radical possessiveness" and thought that when people loved each other they should have the confidence and the trust in each other that would allow them to be independent and strong. Therefore, she reluctantly came to the conclusion that he did not really love her (the "absence makes the heart grow fonder" position).

The issue is not that either the husband is right or the wife is right, or either she is wrong or he is wrong. New formulations appear when the therapist simply substitutes "both/and" for the "either/or" in thinking about the situation. That is, both the husband is right and the wife is right, and both husband and wife are wrong. This leads to a useful problem construction. In this case, the therapist declared both of them to be "right," recognized the validity of both positions, and then expressed his puzzlement: "How can two rights make something so wrong?" (That is, both were right but the results were wrong.) He gave them the following task to see if it might help clear up the puzzle. Simultaneously, they were to take separate walks going in different directions; each one was to spend the time thinking about how he or she was going to make getting back together at the end of the walk pleasantly surprising. (That is, they were to be apart thinking about being together.)

This same intervention was used in each of the four sessions. During the interval between the first and second sessions, they stopped arguing about this issue. Each session they reported progressively coming to value more and more the times when they were reunited after the activities which separated them.

Certainty Rule

Clients, since they are trapped inside the complaint, are usually certain about the details of the complaint and the various elements which make it troublesome. They may not express their thoughts clearly and they may not be able to describe the problem very well, but they are sure about their frames and definitions and meanings. If they were unsure, then they would still be looking for a solution outside of coming to therapy. Therefore, any doubts about any of the elements might be useful. Generally, the "facts" cannot be doubted, but any context might be.

An elderly man reported that he had heard a voice telling him that he was "doomed." Ever since, his wife complained, he just sat there at the front window waiting to die. Month after month he waited, doing nothing even though there was "nothing wrong with him." She had tried to convince him that he had not heard it and that it had been nothing but a dream. Some people, including his doctor, had told him that he was crazy – which he believed, since only crazy people hear voices. The rest of the family joined her in trying to convince him that he was wrong. But he was certain that he was doomed, though he did not know when he would die. She became convinced he was crazy. I asked his wife if he had always been so gullible. She said, "No." I asked because, even though I did not know him yet, I did not think I would want to try selling him a used car. She laughed, saying that it was hard to sell him anything. I said that confirmed my impression, and therefore, I wondered how come he believed what the voice said.

She did not know and neither did he. She was able to tell me about various times when he had not believed things he was told. I pressed the question a bit, again and again wondering how come he chose to believe the voice and made this the theme of the session.

The voice was treated as a matter of "fact"; the only thing to doubt was his believing it. The question no longer was, "Is he crazy?" but rather, "How come he is so gullible?" He came to have some doubts about the voices and began to do some small things in the next two weeks.

Upside Down

Some years ago, I saw a family sent to me by a caseworker who was appalled at their living conditions. Grandfather, father, and two adolescent boys all wet the bed every night; mother daily washed the sheets and blankets. The boys had school problems, grandfather was retired and infirm, and father was on disability. This led the caseworker to see them as a multiproblem family and to describe the whole situation as "hopeless." The visiting nurse was also very concerned about the bed-wetting problem. She had tried to help, but no progress was ever made. The referral sources wanted me to "cure" the bed-wetting (the file on this family was over an inch thick, and bed-wetting was mentioned on every page). The caseworker and the nurse were behind the mirror in the first session and were surprised to hear me start the session by asking mother about her knowledge of sheets, washing machines, bleach and detergents. I quickly found that mother knew a lot about these things and that father was an expert at fixing washers and dryers. Wet beds were never mentioned. I complimented mother on her knowledge and father on his expertise. I suggested to them that all this skill and knowledge were being wasted.

The "bed-wetting" complaints were only half a pattern, one that could not exist without the other half: sheet-washing. The nurse helped mother find a job as a professional laundress (in a nursing home) and father, through the caseworker's help, found a job in a repair shop. Since she no longer had the days available to do laundry at home, the wet beds stopped when grandfather was faced with the task.

Clearly, the complaint itself was only part of a larger pattern (bed-wetting/sheet-washing) that was only half seen. Typically, any repetitive complaint is only the tip of the iceberg. The family was certainly expecting one more helper to focus on the wet beds, but it did not seem useful to me. The pattern can be stood on its head and then the problem can be constructed on a different basis, i.e., when mother no longer washes, then what happens to the wet beds? Clearly, the basis for a spontaneous change is established.

If There Was No "If"

> If there was no "if,"
> There'd be no "stiff";
> He wouldn't be stuck
> With just bad luck*

Poorly constructed problems are usually built around a rather pessimistic idea that change is at least difficult. The word "if" betrays this point of view, which is held by many therapists. Although the other rules of thumb concerned the therapist's listening to the client and thinking about what the client says, this one applies to the therapist's thinking about problem construction and what he says about change. "If" expresses a wish, i.e., "if only things would change," and, therefore, doubt is explicit. But in the context of brief therapy the therapist needs to create the expectation of change, and so the therapist's attitude needs to generally exclude the wish and replace it with certainty. It is not a question of "If change happens?" but "When will it happen?" "When" describes the moment of the event and is not in the least conditional. When a couple or several members of a family are involved in the therapy, then an additional question is, "Who will change

*Charles D. de Shazer, date unknown

first?" In situations with more than one complaint, the therapist might wonder, "Which change might or should happen first?" When the brief therapist talks to clients about change he leaves no room for doubt about its happening.

This is a simple matter of replacing the word "if" with the word "when" during any discussion of change. It is not, "What do you think will happen *if* you two stop fighting?" but rather, "What do you think will happen *when* you two stop fighting?" This is particularly important when working alone, since the team is not there to counteract any conditional statements. The "when" construction firmly puts the therapist on the client's side. When there is a need to be pessimistic about things, the therapist's idea is that the change should or will happen later rather than sooner. Before long, clients and therapists begin to believe it is only a question of, "When will the change happen?"

CONCLUSION

General systems theory and the language of family therapy demand complexity in the description of the system under consideration. Ideas such as recursiveness, self-reflexivity, circularity, non-summativity, wholism, nonlinear causality, relationships within a context, levels of meaning, binds and double binds, loops – strange or otherwise, paradoxes and counterparadoxes have been developed to deal with this complex construction of reality. Added to this are metaphors borrowed from physics, Taoism, Zen, biology, and other special fields. The result is a remarkable theoretical edifice.

Systems

A system can be defined as a complex of elements including the nonrandom relationships between and among those elements and their attributes. Since interactions between elements occur, a time span is implied in this definition. General systems theory is meant to be exactly that: general. It is seen to apply to any system, irrespective of the particular kind of elements and relationships. Of course, this definition leaves open just exactly what is included within the system and what is included in the environment and how to tell the difference.

Hall and Fagan (1956) suggest that

> the relationships to be considered in the context of a given set of objects depend on the *problem at hand*, important or interesting relationships being included, trivial or unessential relationships excluded. The decision as to which relationships are important and which trivial is up to the person dealing with the problem, i.e., the question of triviality turns out to be relative to one's interest (p. 18, emphasis added).

That is, "What is system?" and "What is environment?" are decided by the person dealing with the problem. There are no hard and fast rules for drawing or constructing a boundary between system and environment; it is just a matter of what a person decides to define as "the system under consideration." Any two elements that interact in a nonrandom or patterned fashion can be seen as some sort of a system. These two interacting elements defined as a system might also be defined in a different context, with a different problem, as elements in totally different systems.

The Therapy System

Since the 1950s, the family has been described as fitting the definition of a system, and for almost as long therapy has also been defined as a system. Clearly, therapy is a different kind of system: Unlike the family, it is only temporary and, importantly, it is defined around a problem. The therapy system has a goal and a purpose: solving the problem at hand. Operationally, the therapy system can be defined as including, at least: (1) the therapist, (2) the problem, (3) at least one other person who defines himself as a client, and (4) the relationships between and among the therapist, the problem, and the client.

If different systems are under consideration, then Mrs. Jones might be an element of various systems and labeled as (1) a daughter, (2) a wife, (3) a mother, (4) a sister, or (5) a therapist, etc. Mrs. Jones is part of various organizational wholes, called systems. If she decides to change in some way and/or if she changes spontaneously and/or if she is urged into changing, each of the systems is changed in some way. She is a different daughter to her parents, wife to her husband, etc. In some systems, any particular change might be seen as important while in others it might be seen as trivial. Similarly, to any problem in any of these systems, her interaction might be more or less important or trivial. Thus, who should be in therapy at any one time depends on the relationship each person has to the problem at hand. Mrs. Jones, as wife, may have a problem with her husband, while he does not have a problem with her as wife. Therefore, therapy can be done with just Mrs. Jones and her problem. It can also include Mr. Jones if he wants to work with her on this particular problem, but it should not if he is not interested.

Simplicity

The idea that the therapy system is defined, in part, by the problem allows therapist and client to minimize what otherwise might be bewildering complexity should all these systems be considered equally. Furthermore, this idea allows therapist and client to take advantage of the idea that a change in one person (and/or that one person's relationship with some others) can change the rest of the system under consideration. Which system is the one under consideration is determined by the definition of the problem to be solved.

The previous chapters (and other literature too vast to cite here) describe how the process(es) of change can be initiated. In part, the apparent simplicity is due to what we have learned about initiating change based on more complex constructions or definitions of the therapy system.

Von Glasersfeld's distinction between *match* and *fit* seems particularly relevant in this context.

> The metaphysical realist looks for knowledge that
> *matches* reality [with] . . . some kind of "homomor-
> phism," which is to say, an equivalence of relations,
> a sequence, or a characteristic structure – something,
> in other words, that he can consider *the same*, be-
> cause only then could he say that his knowledge is
> *of* the world (1984a, p. 21).

Fit, however, is quite a different matter.

> If we say that something *fits*, we have in mind a
> different relation. A key fits if it opens the lock. The
> fit describes a capacity of the key, not of the lock
> (p. 21).

In practical terms, if the therapist attempts a match when
thinking about human concerns and complaints or when designing interventions, then the complexity of this edifice can
lead to confusion and chaos. Certainly the insights from systems theory and the conceptual efforts of family therapy give
the therapist a rich repertoire of useful metaphors. The complexity can also lead, on one hand, to paralysis and, on the
other hand, to a sort of random hyperactivity or floundering
around with no end in sight.

This is similar to the situation faced by a painter deciding
which specific green goes on a particular area of his canvas.
There are a multitude of possible greens to pick from and
each green will interact differently with the surrounding colors. He is both blessed and cursed by the variety of greens
that he sees in his mind's eye and the variety of differences
his decision will make in the neighborhood of the green. Ulti-
mately, he can only know which green to choose by doing
something. The more successfully he has made similar decisions before, the more likely it is that the green he picks will
fit. Other painters might find a different green will fit (in
similar neighborhoods), and even the same painter might find
that a different green fits on a different canvas with a similar neighborhood. Even on the same canvas, a variety of
greens might fit, each in differing ways.

The maps of clinical reality presented in the preceding chapters are not meant to be the only maps or to supersede others in a Darwinian "survival of the fittest" map. Various therapeutic maps fit various problem constructions, and other maps might fit as well. The problem can be constructed in a number of ways, and therefore, other fits can be developed that would be as successful. Metaphorically, the same skeleton key can fit various locks, and the same lock can be opened with different keys.

These particular maps fit the assumptions of brief therapy, but these are not the only possible assumptions upon which to map the clinical realities. A structural family therapist (Minuchin, 1974) and a systemic family therapist (Selvini-Palazzoli et al., 1978) will each have a differently constructed map, and therefore, what fits will be different. The poly-ocular view suggests that the various maps, through contrast and comparison — as the left eye's view contrasts with the right's — can produce a bonus, an idea of a higher logical type. This does not make any one set more "right or correct" in any sense, no more so than the right eye's view makes it a "more correct" view than the left eye's.

Importantly, solutions do not depend entirely on either the creativity of the therapist and/or therapy team or of the client. The source of the creativity "lies" in the cooperative relationship between the two subsystems. The creativity is a "bonus" of their poly-ocular view or their various descriptions of the problematic situation. Of course, the therapist's techniques are designed to promote the development of creative solutions, and the creative invention of the most useful techniques in any particular situation is the bonus from the poly-ocular view of the team and/or therapist-client system. This notion is particularly important when the clients' description of their situation is so vague that the therapist cannot get a real picture of the human interaction involved or a clear description of the sequences included in the complaint area. The difference between the clients' more or less negative view (otherwise there would be no complaint) and the therapist's more or less positive view of the same vaguely described situation seems to fit well enough to prompt the bonus.

It seems clear that the concept of fit allows the therapist to construct, with the client, a solution using minimal tools. Fit can be achieved by connecting the intervention with behaviors and/or sequences of behavior and/or the context of the behaviors and/or the frames or meanings given to the behaviors and contexts and/or the more general world view. These various levels seem recursive (mutually defining each other), and therefore, the systemic principle of wholism suggests that a change in one level will affect the other levels. Thus, it is necessary for the concept of fit to be flexible so a problem can be constructed on any, some, or all the various levels. As von Glasersfeld puts it, a fit gives us "*one* viable way to a goal that we have chosen under specific circumstances in our experimental world" (1984a, p. 24), but it tells us nothing about other ways to achieve those goals.

BIBLIOGRAPHY

Adamson, R. E. (1952). Functional fixedness as related to problem solving: A repetition of three experiments. *Journal of Experimental Psychology, 44,* 288-291.

Axelrod, R. (1984). *The evolution of cooperation.* New York: Basic Books.

Axelrod, R., & Hamilton, W. D. (1981). The evolution of cooperation. *Science, 211,* 1390-1396.

Bandler, R., & Grinder, J. (1975). *Patterns of the hypnotic techniques of Milton H. Erickson.* Cupertino: Meta.

Bateson, G. (1979). *Mind and nature: A necessary unity.* New York: Dutton.

Bateson, G., Jackson, D. D., Haley, J., & Weakland, J. (1956). Toward a theory of schizophrenia. *Behavioral Science, 1*(4), 251-264.

Berger, J., Cohen, B., & Zelditch, M. (1966). Status characteristics and expectations states. In J. Berger, M. Zelditch, & B. Anderson (Eds.), *Sociological theories in progress.* Boston: Houghton Mifflin.

Berger, J., Conner, T., & Fisek, M. (1974). *Expectation states theory: A theoretical research program.* Cambridge: Winthrop.

Berger, J., Fisek, M., Norman, R., & Zelditch, M. (1977). *Status characteristics and social interaction: An expectations-state approach.* New York: Elsevier.

Capra, F. (1977). *The Tao of physics.* New York: Bantam.

Castelnuovo-Tedesco, P. (1975). Brief psychotherapy. In D. X. Freedman, & J. E. Dyrud (Eds.), *American handbook of psychiatry* (Vol. 5). New York: Basic.

Coopersmith, E. (Ed.). (1984). *Treatment of families with a handicapped member.* Rockville: Aspen.

Coyne, J. (1984). Strategic therapy with depressed married persons: Initial agenda, themes and interventions. *Journal of Marital and Family Therapy, 10*(1), 53-62.

Cronen, V., Johnson, K., & Lannamann, J. (1982). Paradoxes, double binds, and reflexive loops: An alternative theoretical perspective. *Family Process, 21,* 91-126.

de Shazer, S. (1975a). Brief therapy: Two's company. *Family Process, 14*(1), 78-93.

de Shazer, S. (1975b). The confusion technique. *Family Therapy, 2*(1), 23-30.

de Shazer, S. (1977). The optimist-pessimist technique. *Family Therapy, 4*(2), 93-100.

de Shazer, S. (1978a). Brief hypnotherapy of two sexual dysfunctions: The crystal ball technique. *American Journal of Clinical Hypnosis, 20*(3), 203-208.

de Shazer, S. (1978b). Brief therapy with couples. *International Journal of Family Counseling, 6*(1), 17-30.

de Shazer, S. (1979a). On transforming symptoms: An approach to an Erickson procedure. *American Journal of Clinical Hypnosis, 22*, 17-28.

de Shazer, S. (1979b). Brief therapy with families. *American Journal of Family Therapy, 7*(2), 83-95.

de Shazer, S. (1979c). *The death of resistance.* Unpublished manuscript.

de Shazer, S. (1980a). Brief family therapy: A metaphorical task. *Journal of Marital and Family Therapy, 6*(4), 471-476.

de Shazer, S. (1982a). *Patterns of brief family therapy.* New York: Guilford.

de Shazer, S. (1982b). Some conceptual distinctions are more useful than others. *Family Process, 21*, 71-84.

de Shazer, S. (1984). The death of resistance. *Family Process, 23*, 11-21.

de Shazer, S. & Berg, I. (1984). A part is not apart: Working with only one of the partners present. In A. Gurman (Ed.). *Casebook of marital therapy.* New York: Guilford.

de Shazer, S. & Lipchik, E. (1984). Frames and reframing. In E. Coopersmith (Ed.). *Treatment of families with a handicapped member.* Rockville: Aspen.

de Shazer, S. & Molnar, A. (1984a). Changing teams/changing families. *Family Process, 23*(4).

de Shazer, S. & Molnar, A. (1984b). Four useful interventions in brief family therapy. *Journal of Marital and Family Therapy, 10*(3), 297-304.

de Shazer, S. & Nunnally, E. (1984). The mysterious affair of paradoxes and loops. In G. Weeks (Ed.). *Promoting change through paradoxical techniques.* Homewood, IL: Dow Jones-Irwin.

Duncker, K. (1945). On problem solving. *Psychological monographs, 58.*

Emerson, R. T. & Messinger, S. L. (1977). The micro-politics of trouble. *Social Problems, 25*(2), 121-134.

Erickson, M. H. (1954a). Special techniques of brief hypnotherapy. *Journal of Clinical and Experimental Hypnosis, 2*, 109-129.

Erickson, M. H. (1954b). Pseudo-orientation in time as a hypnotherapeutic procedure. *Journal of Clinical and Experimental Hypnosis, 2,* 261–283.

Erickson, M. H. (1964). The confusion technique in hypnosis. *American Journal of Clinical Hypnosis, 6,* 183–207.

Erickson, M. H. & Rossi, E. (1983). *Healing in hypnosis.* New York: Irvington.

Erickson, M. H., Haley, J., & Weakland, J. (1967). A transcript of a trance induction with commentary. In J. Haley (Ed.). *Advanced techniques of hypnosis and therapy.* New York: Grune & Stratton.

Erickson, M. H. & Rossi, E. (1979). *Hypnotherapy: An exploratory casebook.* New York: Irvington.

Erickson, M. H., Rossi, E., & Rossi, S. (1976). *Hypnotic realities.* New York: Irvington.

Ferrier, M. J. (1984). *Systemic therapy with an individual.* Unpublished manuscript.

Fisch, R. (1983). Personal communication.

Fisch, R., Weakland, J., & Segal, L. (1983). *The tactics of change: Doing therapy briefly.* San Francisco: Jossey-Bass.

Fisher, S. (1980). The use of time limits in brief psychotherapy: A comparison of six-session, twelve-session, and unlimited treatment with families. *Family Process, 19*(4), 377–392.

Fisher, S. (1984). Time-limited brief therapy with families: A one-year follow-up study. *Family Process, 23*(1), 101–106.

Foss, L. (1971). Art as cognitive: Beyond scientific realism. *Philosophy of Science, 38,* 234–250.

Garfield, S. (1978). Research on client variables in psychotherapy. In S. Garfield & A. Bergin (Eds.). *Handbook of psychotherapy and behavior change: An empirical analysis.* New York: Wiley.

Gordon, D. & Meyers-Anderson, M. (1981). *Phoenix: Therapeutic patterns of Milton H. Erickson.* Cupertino: Meta.

Gurman, A. (1981). Integrative marital therapy: Toward the development of an interpersonal approach. In S. Budman (Ed.). *Forms of brief therapy.* New York: Guilford.

Gurman, A. (Ed.). (1984). *Casebook of marital therapy.* New York: Guilford.

Haley, J. (1958). An interactional explanation of hypnosis. *American Journal of Clinical Hypnosis, 1*(2), 41–57.

Haley, J. (1963). *Strategies of psychotherapy.* New York: Grune & Stratton.

Haley, J. (1967a). Commentary on the writings of Milton H. Erickson, M.D. In J. Haley (Ed.). *Advanced techniques of hypnosis and therapy: Selected papers of Milton H. Erickson, M.D.* New York: Grune & Stratton.

Haley, J. (Ed.). (1967b). *Advanced techniques of hypnosis and ther-*

apy: Selected papers of Milton H. Erickson, M.D. New York: Grune & Stratton.

Haley, J. (1973). *Uncommon therapy: The psychiatric techniques of Milton H. Erickson, M.D.* New York: Norton.

Haley, J. (1976). *Problem solving therapy.* San Francisco: Jossey-Bass.

Hall, A. & Fagen, R. (1956). Definition of system. *General systems yearbook, 1,* 18–28.

Heider, F. (1946). Attitudes and cognitive organization. *Journal of Psychology, 21,* 107–112.

Hofstadter, D. R. (1979). *Gödel, Escher, Bach: An eternal golden braid.* New York: Basic Books.

Hofstadter, D. R. (1983). Computer tournaments of the prisoner's dilemma suggest how cooperation evolves. *Scientific American,* May, 16–26.

Koss, M. (1979). Length of psychotherapy for clients seen in private practice. *Journal of Consulting and Clinical Psychology, 47:*210–212.

Kuhn, T. S. (1970). *The structure of scientific revolutions* (2nd ed.). Chicago: University of Chicago Press.

Malan, D. (1976). *The frontier of brief psychotherapy.* New York: Plenum.

Mayer, R. E. (1983). *Thinking, problem solving, cognition.* New York: Freeman.

Mead, G. H. (1934). *Mind, self and society.* Chicago: University of Chicago Press.

Minuchin, S. (1974). *Families and family therapy.* Cambridge: Harvard University Press.

Ouchi, W. (1981). *Theory Z.* Reading, MA:Addison-Wesley.

Rosenthal, R. (1966). *Experimenter effects in behavioral research.* New York: Appleton-Century-Crofts.

Selvini-Palazzoli, M., Boscolo, L., Cecchin, G., & Prata, G. (1974). The treatment of children through brief therapy with their parents. *Family Process, 13,* 429–442.

Selvini-Palazzoli, M., Boscolo, L., Cecchin, G., & Prata, G. (1978). *Paradox and Counterparadox.* New York: Aronson.

Selvini-Palazzoli, M. & Prata, G. (1980). *The prescription.* Paper presented at the Journées Internationales de Therapie Familiale, Lyons, France. Translated by Fabian Daejhsels and Rob Horowitz.

Shibutani, T. (1961). *Society and personality.* Englewood Cliffs: Prentice Hall.

Spiegel, H. & Linn, L. (1969). The "ripple effect" following adjunct hypnosis in analytic psychotherapy. *American Journal of Psychiatry, 126,* 53–58.

Stcherbatsky, F. (1962). *Buddhist logic.* New York: Dover.

Szapocznik, J., Kurtines, W., Foote, F., Perez-Vidal, A., & Hervis, O. (1983). Conjoint versus one-person family therapy: Some evidence for the effectiveness of conducting family therapy through one person. *Journal of Consulting and Clinical Psychology, 51*(6), 889–899.

Tomm, K. (1982). *Clinical applications of strange loops.* Paper presented at the Distinguished Speakers Series, Brief Family Therapy Center, Milwaukee.

von Glasersfeld, E. (1984a). An introduction to radical constructivism. In P. Watzlawick (Ed.). *The invented reality.* New York: Norton.

von Glasersfeld, E. (1984b). *Steps in the construction of "others" and "reality": A study in self-regulation* Paper delivered at the 7th European Meeting on Cybernetics and Systems Research, Vienna.

Watzlawick, P. (1983). *The situation is hopeless but not serious.* New York: Norton.

Watzlawick, P. (Ed.). (1984). *The invented reality.* New York: Norton.

Watzlawick, P., Beavin, J., & Jackson, D. D. (1967). *Pragmatics of human communication.* New York: Norton.

Watzlawick, P., Weakland, J., & Fisch, R. (1974). *Change: Principles of problem formation and problem resolution.* New York: Norton.

Watzlawick, P. & Coyne, J. (1980). Depression following stroke: Brief, problem focused family treatment. *Family Process, 19,* 13–18.

Weakland, J. (1983). "Family therapy" with individuals. *Journal of Strategic and Systemic Therapies, 2*(4), 1–9.

Weakland, J., Fisch, R., Watzlawick, P., & Bodin, A. (1974). Brief therapy: Focused problem resolution. *Family Process, 13,* 141–168.

Webster, M. & Sobieszek, B. (1974). *Sources of self-evaluation: A formal theory of significant others and social influence.* New York: Wiley.

Weeks, G. (Ed.). (1984). *Promoting change through paradoxical therapy.* Homewood, IL: Dow Jones-Irwin.

Weiner-Davis, M. (1984). The road not taken: On knowing what to not do. *Underground Railroad, 5*(1).

Wilden, A. (1980). *System and Structure* (2nd ed.). London: Tavistock.

Wilk, J. (1983). Personal communication.

INDEX

depression (*continued*)
  crystal ball technique used
    for, 94–95
  "do something different" task
    used for, 131–32
  formula task for, 121–22
Derks, Jim, 15*n*, 92*n*
"do something different" task,
  122–32
  case examples of, 125–32
"double binds" (Bateson et al.),
  51–54
  counter double bind "fit" to,
    59–61
  mirror images involved in,
    58–59
drug-use habits:
  double bind/counter double
    bind mapping of, 50–54
  formula task for, 133–34
  strange-loop map of, 54–59
Duncker, K., 39–40

either/or construction, 23–25,
  26–27, 163–64
erectile difficulties:
  crystal ball technique used
    for, 85–87
  goals defining problem in,
    100–104
Erickson, Milton H.:
  arm levitation approach of,
    102
  balance-theoretical view of,
    11
  on client's problem-solving,
    61
  confusion technique of, 9–10
  on cooperation, 79–80, 102
  and crystal ball technique,
    81
  in history of brief therapy,
    5–7
  hypnosis and, 12–13, 35*n*
  law-schema in methods of,
    47–50

"naturalistic techniques" of,
  12–13
on present and future em-
  phasis of therapy, 78
on symptom substitution,
  138–39
on "yes set," 91–92
"exceptions to the rule" (Gingerich and Weiner-Davis),
  34
  certainty rule and, 164–65
  either/or rule and, 23–25, 26–
    27, 163–64
expectations of change, 40, 44–
  46
  client's self-evaluation in, 75,
    98–99
  crystal ball technique and,
    81, 93–94, 137–38
  "do something different" task
    and, 131–32
  in first session formula task,
    137–39, 149–51, 158
  frames and, 40, 74–77, 79
  future as viewed in, 38, 83–
    84, 93–94
  goals and, 44–46
  and others' perceptions of
    client, 42, 82
  present and future emphasis
    and, 78–80
  punctuation in, 43–44, 106
  ripple effect in, 77
  solutions as dependent on,
    45–46, 74–75, 94
"expectation states theory"
  (Berger), 65, 74–77

Fagan, R., 168
family therapy:
  balance-theoretical maps in,
    11
  brief therapy and, 13
  complaints identified in, 27
  complexity as viewed in,
    167

emphasis of elements in,
168-69
family groups as viewed in,
106
hypnotherapy and, 13
relationships involved in,
105-6
single clients as viewed in,
17, 44, 106-8
"system" as viewed in, 106,
167-68
systemic therapists on, 107-8
time element in, 167
wholism in, 43-46; *see also*
wholism, concept of
Szapocznik, J., 107-8

Talley, Jerry, 11*n*
tantrums, "do something different" task used for, 125-
27, 129-31
tasks, *see* first session formula
task; formula tasks; interventions
team approach to therapy, 18-
21
development of, 20-21
mapping by, 19, 27-33, 49-
54
poly-ocular view of, 19-20,
27, 31, 171-72
temptations, overcoming, formula task for, 133-36
therapists:
behavior of, 73, 79-80, 159
client accepted by, 35-36
compliments given by, 91-
92, 116-17
cooperation and role of, 69-
70, 159
expectations of change and,
69-70, 79-80
interventions by, *see* formula tasks; interventions
listening ability of, 90-91
metaphors used by, 12-13,

59-64, 72-73, 167
observer's effect and, 69-70,
73
in response-to-response therapeutic approach, 72-74,
92, 102, 149
in therapy system, 106, 168-
69
therapy:
as collective endeavor, 74-75
interactional activity of, 65-
67, 73
simplicity as possible in, 58,
60-61, 169-70
as system, 106, 168-72
see also brief therapy; couple
therapy; family therapy
TIT FOR TAT (computer
game), 71-74
"tit for tat" therapeutic approach, 109-18
Tomm, K., 54
"Toward a Theory of Schizophrenia" (Bateson et al.),
58-59
trance, client's expectations of,
83
"Treatment of Children Through
Brief Therapy of Their
Parents, The" (Selvini-
Palazzoli et al.), 6-7
"twin stochastic logic" (Bateson), 27

Uncommon Therapy (Haley), 7

victimization, client's sense of,
98-99, 138-39
von Glasersfeld, Ernst:
on concept of fit, 59*n*
on match vs. fit, 46, 61, 119,
169-70

Walter, John, xx, 15*n*
Watzlawick, P., 6-7
on concept of fit, 63-64